Imaging the Bible

Imaging the Bible

*An introduction to
biblical art*

Edited by

MARTIN O'KANE

First published in Great Britain in 2008

Society for Promoting Christian Knowledge
36 Causton Street
London SW1P 4ST

British Library Cataloguing-in-Publication Data
A catalogue record for this book is available from the British Library

ISBN 978–0–281–05897–6

1 3 5 7 9 10 8 6 4 2

Designed and typeset by Kenneth Burnley, Wirral, Cheshire.
Printed in Great Britain by Ashford Colour Press

Produced on paper from sustainable forests

Contents

Contents

List of figures

List of figures

List of plates

(Between pages 142 and 143)

List of contributors

Andreas Andreopoulos is an iconologist and Orthodox theologian, and lectures in Christian Theology at the University of Wales, Lampeter.

Clyde Binfield is Associate Professor of History at the University of Sheffield and former President of the Ecclesiastical History Society.

Sarah Boss is Director of the Centre for Marian Studies at the University of Wales, Lampeter.

Laura Carnevale is Researcher of Ancient Christian History in the Department of Classical and Early Christian Studies at the University of Bari, Italy.

Nicholas Davey is Professor of Philosophy at the University of Dundee.

Peter French is an Anglican priest currently writing a PhD in Art History at the University of Melbourne, Australia.

John Harvey is Professor of Art at the University of Wales, Aberystwyth and Director of the Research Centre for Studies in the Visual Culture of Religion.

Heidi Hornik is Professor of Italian Renaissance and Baroque Art History at Baylor University in Waco, Texas.

John Morgan-Guy is a Research Fellow in the Department of Theology and Religious Studies at the University of Wales, Lampeter.

Martin O'Kane is Director of the research centre The Bible and the Visual Imagination at the University of Wales, Lampeter.

Introduction

In this book on the Bible and art, a number of scholars offer different perspectives on how the visual expression of biblical stories can help the viewer engage more creatively and imaginatively with the text. The idea for such a book began in the research centre The Bible and the Visual Imagination <www.imagingthebible.org> based at the University of Wales, Lampeter, and grew through a series of interdisciplinary seminars which surveyed the different ways in which the Bible has been expressed visually over the centuries. Each short chapter seeks to highlight a distinctive aspect of visual culture and explores how artists have used the Bible as a source of inspiration for quite different ends – not only religious and devotional but also for social and political purposes. A short reading list is provided at the end of each chapter, and a glossary of terms at the end of the book.

The book begins by setting out, with particular reference to the Book of Genesis, how biblical literature itself abounds in vivid descriptions of landscapes, people and events, expressed in language designed to appeal to the reader's visual imagination, and illustrates how such literature translates easily and naturally into painting. Subsequent chapters explore the importance of biblical subjects in early Christian art, in medieval art and in the Italian Renaissance. Three chapters focus on how 'biblical' art served quite different purposes in the Christian Orthodox and Nonconformist traditions, while two further chapters highlight how in modern art reference to biblical subjects tends to become more implicit and subtle. The book concludes with a philosophical appraisal, based on the work of Hans-Georg Gadamer, in which the author argues for the usefulness and appropriateness of hermeneutical approaches that engage with the artist's imaginative interpretation of the biblical narrative.

We have included as many images as is possible in such a small volume. However, the majority of images referred to are generally accessible through a range of useful websites hosted by the art galleries to which the particular paintings belong.

MARTIN O'KANE
University of Wales, Lampeter
January 2008

1

The Bible and the visual imagination

MARTIN O'KANE

The literature of the Bible is highly visual and calls up in the reader's mind colourful images of people, landscapes and events. The Book of Genesis is a particularly fine example where events are recorded and presented vividly and with great immediacy by the biblical authors, firing in turn the imagination of artists through the centuries. In this chapter, Martin O'Kane explores the visual nature of biblical narrative and its appeal to artists.

Introduction

From beginning to end, the Bible abounds in vivid descriptions of landscapes, people and events expressed in language designed to appeal to the reader's visual imagination. It opens with the image of God surveying all his work with the craftsman's eye to detail in Genesis 1 and closes with John's dramatic vision of the new heaven and earth and the new Jerusalem coming down out of heaven from God in Revelation 21. The images we are expected to visualize in our mind's eye are vast in number and demanding in range: from the featureless desert plains of Exodus to the intricate processes of the sowing and harvesting of dill and cummin in Isaiah 28, from the detailed description of Goliath in 1 Samuel 17 to the prophet's

1

startling vision of strange other-worldly creatures in Ezekiel 1. The visual impact becomes even more striking when we look beyond specific texts and explore the overall effect created by the accumulation and interaction of visual images across large sections of literature such as the first five books of the Bible (the Pentateuch) or in the Book of Isaiah. The Pentateuch, for example, from its depiction of the creation of the universe in Genesis 1 to its closing panoramic view of the Promised Land in Deuteronomy 34, becomes a giant canvas on which is painted a whole series of contrasting landscapes – mountains, deserts and seas as well as the moon and stars of the heavens – all of which form an essential backdrop to the narrative. It is the description of the crossing of the Red Sea that creates such a visual impact on our reading of the Exodus story (Exodus 14), the depiction of Mount Sinai that assures a sense of drama and other-worldliness (Exodus 19), the image of desert barrenness that articulates the inner emotions and conflicts of the nomadic Israelites (Exodus 17), the sight of the starry sky at night that convinces Abraham that he will be the father of many nations (Genesis 15.5) and the immediacy of the multi-coloured rainbow that illustrates so vividly the permanence and reliability of the rather abstract theological notion of covenant (Genesis 9.12–14).

Striking, too, is the way aspects we associate with visualization – and with the artistic mind – such as light, space and form are subtly nuanced for maximum effect by the biblical author and how differing degrees of light and darkness, shade and reflection, set the scene and mood of the narrative. For example, the play of light and darkness in the story of Jacob wrestling with the angel is what makes the episode so mysterious and Jacob's adversary seem so obscure (Genesis 32.22–32). While the wide plains of the desert suggest the spaciousness necessary for the travelling hordes on the Exodus journey (Exodus 16), the enclosed space of Sarah's tent is more in keeping with the intimacy surrounding Isaac and Rebekah's marriage (Genesis 24.67). Furthermore, it may well have been the impact of the visual on the imagination of the author that provided the impulse to create the story in the first instance. Scholars now argue convincingly that the visual images contained in many metaphors in the psalms – for example, those relating to 'the wings of Yahweh' (Psalms 17.8; 36.7; 57.1; 61.4; 63.7; 91.4) – were inspired directly by material artefacts. In the light of this, the role of the visual imagination becomes an important factor for consideration both in regard to the original authors of the biblical stories and to their subsequent readers and interpreters.

Paradoxically, however, in spite of the biblical authors' vivid depictions of characters, places and events, at the same time we encounter an unmistakable ambivalence towards, indeed more often a deep suspicion and distrust of, the visual in the Bible, the notion that in the superabundance of pleasurable things to see we must always exercise restraint. We are urged to visualize and explore different ways of seeing, yet the threat of blindness – the inability to see in the Bible's highly visual world, or seeing only dimly and obscurely – is forever present and forcefully articulated. As well as the piercing light of day in which we see clearly, there are also many areas of darkness, obscurity and hiddenness in the Bible that the eye cannot penetrate. The God who is all-seeing prefers to remain out of sight and we are warned sternly against creating any visual likeness of him – yet *he* creates humankind in *his* image; he gives sight and yet makes people blind; he displays the skills of a craftsman and artist, yet he is suspicious and distrustful of humans who mirror the same creativity. What are we to make of this obsession with visibility and hiddenness that permeates the Bible? Why do its authors create stories evidently intended to stimulate and exercise the reader's visual imagination and yet appear so suspicious of the consequences?

The ambiguities and paradoxes associated with seeing in the Bible are so complex that in many instances we can only begin to grasp their significance through the language of metaphor. Metaphor, with its capacity to conceal and hide as well as to reveal and disclose, enables the biblical authors to let us 'see' and imagine what we read while at the same time shielding important details and characteristics, especially those relating to God, from our gaze, rendering them almost invisible or present to us only in dim and obscure ways. It is only through the medium of metaphor that we can begin to understand and articulate the nuances and subtleties associated with sight in the Bible. In addition, metaphor is fundamental not only to our understanding of language but also to our appreciation of the visual arts; it provides that common ground between text and image that helps us explore the parallel processes at work in the way a reader draws out the telling silences from a text and the viewer what lies hidden or subtly obscured in a biblical painting. The potential of a biblical painting to reveal something new about the text it seeks to depict or illustrate is something that I will return to later in this chapter with specific reference to the troublesome episode of the deception of Isaac.

The Bible and its visual expression

Considering the rich visual language used by its authors, it is hardly surprising that the stories people remember best from the Bible are those that are most striking visually. Old Testament scholar Cheryl Exum notes:

> It is not simply a matter of the Bible influencing culture; the
> influence takes place in both directions. What many people
> know or think they know about the Bible often comes more
> from familiar representations of biblical texts and themes in
> popular culture than from the study of the ancient text itself . . .
> Not only will our knowledge of the biblical text influence the
> way we view, say, a painting of a biblical scene, our reading of
> the biblical text is also likely to be shaped by our recollection of
> that painting.[1]

It is virtually impossible to read or listen to a familiar biblical passage, from either the Old or the New Testament, without calling to mind a visual representation of it in a church, an art gallery or film (and, of course, access to a wide variety of 'biblical' paintings from all ages and places has now been made possible by the ever-increasing number and quality of art websites). Our reading and understanding of biblical stories are frequently influenced by our encounter with and response to the cultural, and in particular the visual, afterlives of the narrative. Often, the lack of detail in a terse biblical narrative invites us to expand or enhance the story in our imagination and we look to the artist's interpretation to fill out and complete the details of the unsatisfactorily short narrative. The artistic afterlives of biblical characters provide opportunities to question the text and the motives of its author, and encourage us to read the passage again more imaginatively and acknowledge the range of possibilities and different perspectives from which the text may be understood and interpreted.

Throughout Christian tradition, to separate the biblical word from the visual image was simply unthinkable for both believer and artist. The importance of internal visual representation of biblical scenes from the thirteenth century onwards was seen as an indispensable aid to prayer and meditation. The anonymous text *Giardino de orationi* (Garden of Prayer), written in 1454 and widely available during the fifteenth and sixteenth centuries, instructed the faithful how best to meditate upon and remember the story of the Passion. It advised them to make a memory place of their own familiar surroundings in order to visualize the successive events of the Passion to be remembered in various locations within that space:

> The better to impress the story of the Passion on your mind
> and to memorise each action of it more easily, it is helpful and
> necessary to fix the places and people in your mind: a city for
> example will be the city of Jerusalem – taking for this purpose
> a city that is well known to you . . . and then too you must

shape in your mind some people, well known to you, to represent for you the people involved in the Passion . . .[2]

This spiritual exercise was readily translated into paint (as indeed was the case in many Renaissance paintings), the best example being the depiction of *The Passion* in Turin by the early Netherlandish painter Memling (c. 1440–94), which is, in effect, an illustration of the advice of the handbook. Creating a visual continuous narrative of Gospel events that corresponded to the lives of an illiterate faithful was of the utmost importance. The painter was regarded as 'a professional visualizer of the holy stories' and his pious public were practised in spiritual exercises that demanded a high level of visualization of the central episodes in the life of Jesus. American art scholar David Freedberg demonstrates, with illustrations from the Passion of Christ, how the imaginative intensity of Gospel passages was greatly increased by painters 'to arouse the empathetic responses necessary for successful meditation',[3] particularly through artists' attempts to depict the psychological and emotional traits of important biblical characters.

Ignatius of Loyola (1491–1556), founder of the Jesuit Order, in his *Spiritual Exercises* urged his followers to engage in visual contemplation of biblical texts, 'to see from the view of the imagination' the physical place and characters of the scene, as Italian author Italo Calvino (1923–85) puts it:

The believer was called upon personally to paint frescoes crowded with figures on the walls of his mind, starting out from the stimuli that his visual imagination succeeds in extracting from even the most laconic verse from the gospels.[4]

Catholicism of the Counter-Reformation, the period of revival of the mid sixteenth to seventeenth centuries, had already possessed a fundamental vehicle in its ability to use visual communication: through the emotional stimuli of sacred art, the believer was supposed to grasp the meaning of the verbal teachings and biblical doctrines of the Church. But it was always a matter of starting from a *given* image, one proposed and sanctioned by the Church and not 'imagined' by the individual believer. What distinguishes Ignatius's approach is the shift from the word to the visual image as a way of attaining knowledge 'of the most profound meaning' and his attempt to open up a field of infinite possibilities in the way the individual imagination depicted biblical characters, places and scenes in motion.

Different approaches to using 'biblical' art

Encouraged by biblical scholars such as Robert Alter and J. P. Fokkelman, we have now become more attuned to the Bible's literary subtleties and nuances – and less preoccupied with its historical and theological perplexities – but we still pay scant attention to the visual imagery contained in the narrative and to the way its language is designed to appeal to the reader's visual imagination. A glance at recent book titles from other disciplines, however, confirms the surge of interest in the cultural interpretation of biblical themes in art, music, literature and film. They illustrate how some of the most exciting, engaging and creative insights into biblical narrative – especially concerning the representation of biblical characters – now come from authors and researchers based not in traditional theology-related disciplines but in the areas of literature, history of art, music and media studies. For instance, Jean-Paul Kauffmann's *Wrestling with the Angel: The Mystery of Delacroix's Mural* (London: The Harvill Press, 2003) explores how the famous mural in the church of Saint-Sulpice in Paris reveals new and unexpected insights into the mysterious episode from Genesis 32. Paolo Berdini, in *The Religious Art of Jacopo Bassano: Painting as Visual Exegesis* (Cambridge: Cambridge University Press, 1997) explains how and why painting became such an important medium in communicating the type of biblical exegesis favoured during the period of the Counter-Reformation. Nissan N. Perez, in *Revelation: Representations of Christ in Photography* (London: Merrell Publishers, 2003), demonstrates how contemporary artists frequently allude to well-known iconic images, such as Michelangelo's *Last Supper*, in their work.

Nevertheless, there are signs that, increasingly, visual interpretations of biblical texts are being included in contemporary commentaries and other publications related to the Bible, that affirm and value the rich and varied afterlives these texts have enjoyed (for example, the Blackwell Bible Commentaries series emphasizes the influence of the Bible on literature, art, music and film). In some cases, they are used to draw out the devotional and doctrinal aspects of a biblical theme envisaged by the artist (for example, John Drury, *Painting the Word* (New Haven: Yale University Press, 1999)), in other cases to explore the appropriation of texts in specific historical and political contexts (Richard C. Trexler, *The Journey of the Magi: Meanings in History of a Christian Story* (Princeton: Princeton University Press, 1997)). Frequently they offer starting points, or are used as evidence for positions already taken up, in gendered readings of the text (Mieke Bal, *Reading 'Rembrandt': Beyond the Word–Image Opposition* (Cambridge: Cambridge University Press, 1991)). But, given the vast and overwhelming range of visual interpretations now accessible to the contemporary biblical commentator, how does one select images or paintings that shed new insights into the meaning and significance of the text, and in particular, that foreground those aspects otherwise lost, or insufficiently brought out, in traditional or current exegesis? Is the selection of paintings used to illustrate the significance of a text merely arbitrary, and limited to the range of paintings familiar to the commentator and to his or her academic or personal interests? In what sense does a 'biblical' painting illumine a biblical text and what credibility or authority does an artist or painting really bring to the task of interpretation?

Some argue that biblical paintings, in the traditional art-historical mould, do little to support contemporary, inclusive and explorative readings of the text; others question whether modern art with its essentially abstract approach can convey any identifiable cultural afterlife of the narrative, given that artistic subjectivity rather than the biblical iconographical traditions of past centuries is central to its approach (Gesa E. Thiessen, *Theology and Modern Irish Art* (Dublin: Columba Press, 1999)). When art is used to enhance, expand or comment on a biblical text, the dynamic between the written text, the visual expression of its subject matter and the viewer comes to the fore, raising in turn issues of a philosophical nature such as the word–image order, the relationship between a text (what is written) and an image (what is seen), and whether it is even possible to reduce what we see in a painting to the level of verbal explication rather than concentrate on its sheer (inarticulable) sensibility. To these considerations, we might add the question of what contribution the analyses of visual expressions of biblical subject matter make to the ongoing dialogue between art and the broader theological agenda.

While many biblical commentators now focus on the dynamic that takes place between the written biblical text and its reader (D. Marguerat and Y. Bourquin, *How to Read Bible Stories* (London: SCM Press, 1999)), there has been much less interest in engaging with approaches that explore how the involvement of the viewer in the biblical visual image determines its meaning and significance. It is our response as viewers, or the response that the artist intends to elicit from the viewer, that helps us discover unexpected subtleties in the parallel biblical text. Traditionally, the role of the patron (church, secular and political authorities or individuals of power and influence) has played a major part in determining how a biblical text should be visually expressed; despite this, however, the patron cannot control or determine the effect a painting has had on its viewers living in different times and cultures. We need to explore further the processes at work in a painting's engagement of its viewer in biblical subject matter and accentuate the role of the artist as an active *reader* of the Bible and not merely an illustrator of biblical scenes. Understanding the process at work between a biblical painting and its viewer – and seeing this process in parallel terms to what happens between a biblical text and its reader – allows us to appreciate how the painting of a biblical subject presents to the viewer an event in which he or she becomes involved and how different visual instances of the same subject matter broaden the horizons of the viewer.

Two seminal studies provide the theoretical and hermeneutical groundwork in this regard. In 'The Question of Truth as it Emerges from the Experience of Art' in his magnum opus, *Truth and Method*, the philosopher Hans-Georg Gadamer sets out the role of hermeneutical aesthetics in understanding the function of art.[5] In his extended theoretical introduction 'Scripture Reading and Visual Exegesis' in *The Religious Art of Jacopo Bassano: Painting as Visual Exegesis,* art historian Paolo Berdini deals with the processes at work when an artist paints a biblical scene and argues that what is visualized is not the text but a reading of the text, a process he calls 'visual exegesis'.[6] Applying both approaches to the visualization of biblical subject matter illumines the key role given to the viewer in the visual hermeneutical process. In Chapter 10 of this book, philosopher Nicholas Davey presents the work of Gadamer, showing how his approach provides the theoretical framework that underscores the worth and value of 'visual exegesis'; but, here, a specific case study of a painting of Genesis 27 by the seventeenth-century Dutch artist Matthias Stom amply illustrates the richness of his approach.

The deception of Isaac (Genesis 27)

Visual representations serve to question and challenge the stereotypes and assumptions often made about characters in so many biblical commentaries. In paintings of biblical scenes, it is the artist's handling of the complexities of the key characters that makes the painting so compelling and this is certainly true, for example, of Rembrandt's *Bathsheba* or Rubens's *Delilah*, as Cheryl Exum has so well illustrated.[7] Genesis 27, with its range of contrasting characters, its many ambiguities and portrayal of the more disturbing sides of human nature, provides a further example of an Old Testament text that held a universal and irresistible appeal for artists, especially in the seventeenth century.

The dramatic story of the deception of Isaac in Genesis 27 reflects the skill of the biblical author in profiling four important characters: Isaac, Rebekah, Jacob and Esau. The chapter oscillates dangerously between the stark realities of death and life. At the start of the chapter, Isaac is on the brink of death (v. 2) and, at the end, Jacob's life is seriously threatened by Esau (v. 41). Rebekah reflects that her life will 'be of no good to her' if Jacob marries a Hittite woman (v. 46). But the theme of life is also present through the promise of the blessing (mentioned seven times), a blessing given by Isaac to Jacob. Life and blessing are associated with Jacob, to whom God gives the dew of heaven and the fatness of the earth (v. 28) while death and oblivion are reserved for Isaac, Esau and Rebekah. The author creates a plot involving four characters who either perpetrate, or are the victims of, an intricate web of deception: the patriarch Isaac, his wife Rebekah and their twin sons, Esau and Jacob. The context of the story makes the deception even more poignant considering that Rebekah is introduced to the reader in Genesis 24 in one of the most imaginative and romantic stories in ancient literature and a popular subject in art: for example, Castiglione's *Rebekah Led by the Servant of Abraham* (Plate 1), in which the artist depicts Rebekah turning her back, literally, on her own people to embrace the life and people of Isaac.

By the end of the chapter there is no doubt in the reader's mind that Rebekah is indeed a most suitable wife for Isaac (v. 67). When it is apparent that she is barren, he prays to the Lord for her (Genesis 25.21) and their affection for each other is highlighted in 26.8 where Isaac is seen 'fondling his wife'. In the story of deceit in Genesis 27, however, there is no direct or immediate contact between them. In a chapter full of dialogue, only in the very last verse does Rebekah address her husband (v. 46) – and only here to express her concern about finding a wife for Jacob. This is the last we see or hear of Rebekah: that her final appearance should involve such an act of deception contrasts sharply with the way she is first introduced. The optimism and romanticism of Genesis 24, underscored by the central motif of a journey and the setting off into a future of promise and hope, are replaced by the manipulation, partiality, deceit and treachery of Genesis 27, underscored by the setting of a deathbed scene – yet another departure, but this time to death and eternal separation.

Whereas Rebekah is portrayed as powerful and manipulative, Isaac is portrayed as weak and ineffectual, lying in bed, weak and blind, while others act on him; manipulated by his father in his youth (Genesis 22) and by his wife in his old age. Jacob is presented as a liar whose only anxiety is that his deceit might be uncovered (Genesis 27.12). The calculating and deceptive nature of Jacob (Genesis 25.29–34) contrasts with the openness and spontaneity of the character of Esau (Genesis 25.30; 27.38). The reader is thus presented with a dysfunctional family, full of division and partiality, a family that by the end of Genesis 27 is torn apart. The narrative is brilliantly constructed, not only in the psychological portrayals of its characters but equally in its deliberate silences and the many unanswered questions it raises for the reader: how can Isaac, as part of the patriarchal trio, Abraham, Isaac and Jacob, be regarded by posterity with the same respect as Abraham and Jacob when he is presented here in such a weak and ineffectual manner? How can Esau, as the firstborn, be treated so unfairly? Is Rebekah, the only female in the narrative, presented in a negative way simply to ensure the continuation of the biblical stereotype of the woman as seductress and deceiver? But most of all, how can God act through such deceit to bring about his plans?

In Genesis 27, the narrator insinuates the reader, an innocent bystander, into the narrative by inviting him or her to identify with the characters of the plot. An effective technique to draw the reader into the story is the creation of a plot that is centred around the five senses. This ensures that the story has an immediate and universal appeal and that the reader is brought close to the characters in a very tangible way – she or he can almost see, hear, touch, feel and smell them. Isaac cannot see (v. 1) and so he must rely on his other senses of taste (vv. 4, 25), touch (vv. 21, 22, 26, 27) and smell (v. 27) but yet ignores the evidence from what he hears (v. 22). Rebekah's success, on the other hand, comes from her sense of hearing: she listens in to Isaac's conversation with Esau (vv. 5–6), and she urges Jacob to listen to her advice and plans (vv. 8, 13, 43). As well as an appeal to the senses, the emotions of the characters are brought into play. Jacob expresses fear that he may be caught (vv. 11–12), Isaac trembles violently when Esau returns (v. 33), Esau cries out and weeps (vv. 34, 38), he is furious with rage (v. 45) and hates his brother (v. 41). While the appeal to the senses makes the characters credible and the scene almost tangible, the detailed reporting of such emotional anguish demands our spontaneous reaction and judgement on the scene – the emotions experienced by the characters are transmitted to the reader. Such drama, passion and pathos, as we shall see, translated easily from literature into painting.

Artistic representations of Genesis 27

The theme of Isaac blessing Jacob appears occasionally in early Christian, Byzantine and medieval art but it comes into prominence only in the Renaissance and the seventeenth century, the most famous Renaissance treatments of the subject being Ghiberti's relief on the doors of the Baptistery in Florence (c. 1439) and Raphael's fresco in the Loggia of the Vatican (1518–19). Surprisingly, though, Rembrandt never actually painted the episode and when depicting a patriarchal blessing from the Old Testament, he chose instead the subject of Jacob blessing the sons of Joseph (Genesis 48). The reason for this choice is that Rembrandt preferred to present the character of the idealized Old Testament patriarch in a positive and reverential way; in Genesis 27, the aged father Isaac is deceived as a result of his blindness and infirmity, but in the story of Jacob blessing the sons of Joseph in Genesis 48, the venerable patriarch Jacob is gifted with superior knowledge and intuition when he chooses to bless Ephraim rather than his brother Manasseh. However, other painters of the period were much less concerned to protect the character of Isaac and less reticent to portray the deceitful nature of Rebekah.

Matthias Stom, *Isaac Blessing Jacob* (c. 1633–40)

Very little is known about Matthias Stom, an almost invisible figure in the annals of the history of art, except that he was a prolific seventeenth-century Dutch artist who worked mostly in Italy and that of his nearly 200 paintings that survive, three-quarters depict biblical subjects. In *Isaac Blessing Jacob* (Plate 2), which purports to depict very specifically the moment of deception (Genesis 27.21–23), the arrangement of the characters is such that the viewer, standing in front of the painting, is effectively drawn into the event and the emotional intensity of the scene.

The setting consists of a bed upon which the aged Isaac reclines surrounded by Jacob and Rebekah; this is illuminated from the right by a shaft of light which floods the scene, poignantly emphasizing the blind old man who seems oblivious to it. Disconcerted with Jacob's voice, Isaac has beckoned to him to come closer so that he may feel his hands and assure himself that they are those of Esau. His suspicions allayed, the frail Isaac prepares to bestow the blessing. Rebekah raises her finger, warning the viewer not to divulge the deceit.

Jacob's fear is portrayed through his anxious expression and divided pose, for although his hands move forward with the meal his feet appear rooted to the ground; this ambivalent attitude summarizes his eagerness to receive the blessing yet his fear of detection. Even the leaping dog may be interpreted as part of the conspiracy – it may be intended as impersonating one of Esau's hunting dogs, thereby clinching the deception. Isaac is presented as a gaunt and wasted figure who gropes poignantly into space seeking to establish contact with his son. His semi-nakedness adds to his vulnerability and contrasts with the costumes of Rebekah and Jacob: Rebekah wears an elaborate headdress decorated with pearls, while the overdressed Jacob sports a red waistcoat and silver doublet tied with blue ribbons, slashed red breeches and a magnificently plumed hat. Through his attire, Jacob openly declares to the viewer (but not to his father) that he has donned a disguise. The semi-naked Isaac, in contrast, is presented without any suitable bedding and is given only a plain black background.

Stom, like the biblical author, implicates the viewer in the deception. The depiction of the three biblical figures in a semi-circle suggests a certain incompleteness – only when the viewer closes the circle is the act of deception accomplished. The viewer stands in close proximity to the three figures and directly opposite Rebekah, who stares back and raises her finger, urging us not to alert Isaac to the crime being perpetrated. The curtain pulled aside suggests the darkness and secrecy of the deed to which only the viewer is privy – one feels that were the curtain to fall behind the viewer, he or she would become even more complicit in the secrecy of the crime. As in the biblical narrative, the senses are highlighted: in particular, the sense of sight – Rebekah holds the viewer in a fixed stare while Jacob's eager but fearful eyes are contrasted with Isaac's lack of sight. The emphasis on the sense of touch is almost tangible: Jacob's hands covered with goatskin are within reach of the viewer but it is the movement of Isaac's arm as he reaches over to touch Jacob that particularly catches the eye. Isaac's arm, stretching across the centre of the painting and just below Rebekah's finger of deception, unites the figures of Isaac and Jacob. This has the effect of focusing the viewer's attention on the two characters – father and son, old age and youth, one blind and one with vivid sight, one partially naked and one fully and magnificently clothed. Even though the faces of Rebekah and her favourite son are in very close proximity, suggesting a commonality of purpose, the stretched arm of Jacob creates a more formal unity for the viewer to contemplate. In several other paintings, one frequently finds that the hand or arm acts as an arrow directing the viewer's attention to the most important feature or theme of the painting. In this case, the eye follows Isaac's arm and rests on the character of Jacob.

Seen within this perspective, the theme moves from one of human deception to contemplation of a wider divine plan. Jacob is no longer seen as the deceiver of his aged, frail father but as the inheritor of the promise, the leader now entrusted to take over from him. His magnificent clothes now remind the viewer of a prince, a nobleman in whom divine authority is invested.

The figure of Jacob as one invested with divine authority is further highlighted if we consider the two paintings that were originally intended to accompany this one. *Isaac Blessing Jacob* was one of three paintings commissioned by an unknown patron, probably in Naples in the 1630s, and together with *Tobias Healing his Father's Blindness*, it was intended to flank a centrepiece *Christ Disputing with the Doctors*. All three paintings originally formed a devotional narrative triptych. The composition of the first two canvases is comparable, with the fathers and youths and the motif of the leaping dog. The theme of the triptych is the confrontation between old age and youth, illustrated by three examples taken from the Old and New Testaments and the Apocrypha: it concerns the dependence of old age upon youth, either for perpetuation (Jacob), instruction (Christ) or healing (Tobias), and the passing of authority and power from old age to youth.

The contrast between Isaac blessing Jacob and Tobias healing his father Tobit's blindness is very striking. The figure of Tobit to the left of the picture resembles that of Isaac, Tobias resembles the figure of Jacob and the angel Raphael initiating and guiding the process of healing replaces the figure of Rebekah and her plot to deceive. The leaping dog in *Isaac Blessing Jacob* serves to link the story with that of Tobias (Tobit 6.2). Rather than taking advantage of an old man's blindness as Jacob does, Tobias displays his compassion in seeking to restore his father's sight (Tobit 11.10–15). The hand of Tobit is held up in recognition and gratitude as the scales fall from his eyes while Isaac's hand flounders in darkness, ignorance and confusion. These two paintings, on either side of the centrepiece, offer contrasting aspects of the relationship between a father and son and the obvious comparison between Tobias and Jacob serves to make Jacob's crime appear even more heinous.

In *Isaac Blessing Jacob*, the flaws in Jacob's character are set out clearly and unambiguously, but it would also seem that his character is partially rehabilitated when we view this painting alongside the two others that make up the triptych. The young Jacob is seen alongside the young Tobias and the young Christ; just as the plans and designs of God are kept hidden from the aged Tobit and the aged doctors of the law, so too his plans are concealed from Isaac. God's affirmation of the young Tobias and the young Christ reminds us of his choice of Jacob, reflected in his elegant clothing that bestows on him the presence and aura of a prince, someone who is worthy of the authority and trust that God invests in him.

First impressions of Stom's *Isaac Blessing Jacob* might suggest that the artist is interested in portraying only the human psychological drama of the biblical narrative of Genesis 27, by appealing chiefly to the senses and emotions, but the painting also allows us to move from character to character evaluating their role not only in this scene but also in the roles that history has given them. It allows us to explore the interrelationship between the characters: Rebekah's relationship with her favourite son, Isaac's relationship with his successor Jacob, and the final stages of the relationship between Isaac and Rebekah that had begun so romantically but ends so deceptively.

On the surface, there is nothing positive or wholesome in this painting: bedridden old age and a scheming mother and son. But the painting does raise several searching questions: where and how in this peculiar set of relationships is God present? How can God act through deceitful ways? How does God act in the complicated web of human relationships that make up life? The lack of any background objects and the focus on light and darkness suggest that such questions not only relate to this painting but are applicable to all times and places. The Bible speaks with many voices and unsatisfactory or inexplicable episodes have not been censored or excluded. It lets us see all sides to life – the uncomfortable and darker sides of human nature as well as the more exalted and heroic. Biblical literature, like painting, exposes us to the raw reality of life and encourages us to deal with it in all its complexity. However, the placing of this particularly troubling episode from Genesis 27 within a triptych that features scenes from apocryphal and New Testament literature tones down the negative implications of Genesis 27 by counterbalancing the character of Jacob against two positive images, those of Tobias and Christ. The intention, perhaps, is to encourage the viewer to balance negative aspects of human nature alongside more positive ones and to justify, especially where God is concerned, why the end really does justify the means.

The role of the imagination

A final, if brief, word must be said about the role of the imagination in exegesis (the cognate term 'image' lies at the heart of the word 'imagination') since the importance of the imagination in reading biblical texts has never been sufficiently highlighted. We rely on the imagination of artists to provide original and creative afterlives for the text but the reader too must exercise his or her visual imagination in order to appreciate fully, be persuaded by, the Bible's plots and characters. Theologian Michael Austin notes that too often the imagination is identified with the untrammelled, ill-disciplined, irrational part of us. The imagination, he argues, is not opposed to the intellect – it does not go against reason: 'While reason leads to construct systems and employ arguments, the imagination compels us to paint pictures and tell stories and create myths, to recognize and value apparent disorder.'[8]

The Italian poet Dante (1265–1321), for whom there was a kind of luminous source in the skies that transmits images, speaks most passionately of the role of the imagination in *The Divine Comedy* (Canto XVII.13–18):

> Imagination is that which has the power to impose itself upon
> our faculties and our wills, stealing us away from the outer
> world and carrying us off into an inner one, so that even if a
> thousand trumpets were to sound, we would not hear them.

In reading the Bible, we, too, often neglect the importance of the visual imagination in our hermeneutical processes. In bringing more insights from the world of visual culture to bear on the way we engage with and interpret the biblical text, we will surely find that it can reveal new, original and unexpected riches in terms both of its characters and of its plots.

Notes

1 J. Cheryl Exum, *Plotted, Shot, and Painted: Cultural Representations of Biblical Women* (Gender, Culture, Theory, 3; JSOTSup, 215; Sheffield: Sheffield Academic Press, 1996), pp. 7–8.

2 Cited in Lew Andrews, *Story and Space in Renaissance Art: The Birth of Continuous Narrative* (Cambridge: Cambridge University Press, 1995), p. 29.

3 David Freedberg, *The Power of Images: Studies in the History and Theory of Response* (Chicago: University of Chicago Press, 1989), p. 168.

4 Italo Calvino, *Six Memos for the Next Millennium* (London: Random House, 1996), p. 86.

5   Hans-Georg Gadamer, *Truth and Method* (London: Sheed & Ward, 1975), pp. 5–150.
6   P. Berdini, *The Religious Art of Jacopo Bassano: Painting as Visual Exegesis* (Cambridge: Cambridge University Press, 1997).
7   J. Cheryl Exum, *Plotted, Shot, and Painted.*
8   Michael Austin, *Explorations in Art, Theology and the Imagination* (London: Equinox, 2005), p. 2.

Suggested reading

Michael Austin, *Explorations in Art, Theology and the Imagination* (London: Equinox, 2005).
Graham Howes, *The Art of the Sacred: An Introduction to the Aesthetics of Art and Belief* (London: I.B. Tauris, 2007).
Martin O'Kane, *Painting the Text: The Artist as Biblical Interpreter* (Sheffield: Sheffield Phoenix Press, 2007).

2

The Bible and early Christian art

LAURA CARNEVALE

It is clear that biblical episodes were depicted in art from the earliest Christian centuries. Laura Carnevale explores how themes from both the Old and New Testaments provided artists and their patrons with vital inspiration for their art-work; in particular, they selected texts and biblical events that could be easily appropriated for use in cemeteries and eucharistic gatherings in the first Christian centuries.

Introduction

The origins of Christian art in the West can be traced to the late second and early third centuries CE. The earliest examples consisted of the decoration of the underground burial places, or catacombs, in pro-consular Africa, Malta, Syracuse and Naples, but especially in Rome. Subsequently, between the end of the third and the beginning of the fourth century, Christian art found another field of expression in the sculptured reliefs of the sarcophagi. This might lead us to assume that, initially, all the manifestations of Christian art in the West were to be found in a strictly funerary context. We must keep in mind, however, that the catacombs were underground cemeteries used for the burial of the faithful and not, as is sometimes thought, for meetings, which would have required larger, airier spaces. Such meetings took place in private houses, called *domus ecclesiae* (house-churches), provided by wealthy members of the Christian community. As regards the burial of the deceased, prior to the use of catacombs, the Christians buried their own dead alongside pagans in mixed cemeteries.

For the purposes of this chapter, I will confine my discussion of early Christian art to the city of Rome. The iconography attested to in Roman cemeteries, apart from being considerably more extensive than in other early Christian centres, has notable affinities with figurative representations in sepulchres and cemeteries elsewhere in the wider Roman world, as well as with the paintings in the *domus ecclesia* of Dura Europos.[1] It was in Rome, indeed, that all the various aspects of the Christian world came together; Rome provides us with the most comprehensive archaeological, iconographic and epigraphic documentation of early Christianity available.

One of the oldest Roman catacombs is that of Callixtus, which takes its name from the pope of the same name (217–22). While still a deacon, Callixtus was appointed by Pope Zephyrinus (199–217) to administer a huge cemetery area that belonged to the Church, along the old Appian Way. The catacomb of Callixtus thus became the first communal Christian cemetery known definitively to have been run by a member of the hierarchy, who was responsible for organizing the burials and selecting the iconography that satisfied the doctrinal and catechetical requirements of the community. The structure and organization of the catacomb of Callixtus, therefore, provide historical evidence of an important turning point in the Roman Church, which began to take on a unitary and centralized structure from the early third century onwards. This had major repercussions on all aspects of community life, not least on iconography: from the mid third century onwards, there is evidence of hierarchical ecclesiastical control over the choice and portrayal of iconographic themes. However, we must also remember that so-called 'private' catacombs existed as well, which were quite distinct from those in community cemeteries. In 'private' catacombs, the themes and subjects of the artistic repertory were chosen not by the hierarchy but by those responsible for commissioning the paintings, often members of influential families, whose preference was often for subjects other than those easily recognizable images in common use during this period. Divergence from the more general iconographic themes can be explained by a number of factors: for example, a desire to represent a distinct personal spirituality, a preference for certain biblical books or characters, or a desire to express particular religious concepts. An example of a 'private' catacomb is the so-called 'anonymous catacomb' on the Via Latina, uncovered by Father Antonio Ferrua in 1955–7 and dated to approximately the early fourth century. Unusual biblical subjects, not found in the standard early iconographical repertory, occur here: for example, the appearance of the three men to Abraham by the oak of Mamre (Genesis 18.1–15), Jacob's dream (Genesis 28.10–15), episodes from the story of Samson (Judges 15–16), Jesus and the Samaritan woman at the well (John 4.4–26), and Jesus flanked by Saints Peter and Paul. Interesting, too, is the presence of mythological scenes, images that derive from figurative pagan production, such as the goddess Tellus, Ceres and Hercules and the depiction of an anatomy lesson. The co-existence of pagan and Christian themes has been interpreted as an indication of the religious syncretism found in some cultivated parts of the world during Late Antiquity. This syncretism reflects the particular composition of the Roman aristocracy during the fourth century: members of the same family could be followers either of pagan cults or of Christianity and therefore, with regard to their burial within the same sepulchral place, they were at liberty to request the portrayal of subjects and decorative motifs that reflected concepts and ideals linked to their own particular beliefs.

With regard to early Christian cemeterial art, it should be strongly emphasized that most of the catacombs would appear to have been created for community burials. It would be a mistake, however, to think that all the catacombs were covered with frescoes. In actual fact, paintings were only to be found in a few rooms; most of the spaces generally seem to have been bare. This is also a reflection of the far from thriving financial situation of the early Christian communities: the cost of frescoing a catacomb wall or of carving reliefs onto a sarcophagus must have been quite significant. However, even today, the cemeterial paintings that survive have much to offer scholars – not just iconographic experts but also iconologists and art historians – in terms of information regarding the lives of the early Christians, the doctrines they professed, their level of culture and their familiarity with the Bible. Of special interest are the iconographical subjects that were particularly popular during the first few centuries of Christianity and the relationship between these forms of artistic expression and their main source of inspiration, the Bible.

Iconographical subjects in early Christianity

Early Christian art focused initially on the 'Shepherd' and the *Orans* (the praying figure), the two subjects depicted most frequently in the oldest sections of the catacombs in Rome (in some of the rooms in the catacombs of Callixtus, Priscilla and Domitilla, see Figure 1). As in much of the Early Christian iconographical repertory, the figurative tradition of these two characters is connected with pagan art. Scholars now believe that, before being incorporated into Christian art, the two figures were present in pagan pastoral idyllic scenes and were used generally to represent the concepts of philanthropy (on the part of the gods) and of *pietas* (on the part of humans). In line with typical early Christian practice, the symbolism of these subjects underwent a change: while their iconographical form remained unchanged, they assumed a different meaning and significance. The image of the Shepherd was now associated with a series of biblical passages: the story of the Good Shepherd (John 10.1–21) and the Parable of the Lost Sheep, referred to both in Matthew (18.12–14) and in Luke (15.4–6). Various Old Testament texts provided references to the praying figure, the *Orans*: for example, Exodus 17.11 ('As long as Moses held up his hands, the Israelites were winning, but whenever he lowered his hands, the Amalekites were winning'); Lamentations 3.41 ('Let us lift up our hearts and our hands to God in heaven'); Psalm 119.48 ('My hands also will I lift up unto thy commandments, which I have loved; and I will meditate on thy statutes'). In the New Testament, the *Orans* represented a well-known Pauline passage on prayer: 1 Timothy 2.8 ('I want men everywhere to lift up holy hands in prayer, without anger or disputing'). The Shepherd is shown as a male character standing near the sheep, sometimes carrying a sheep on his shoulders; the *Orans* can be a male or female character (probably the deceased) or a biblical character depicted in a standing position with arms outstretched (the so-called *expansis manibus* attitude). The images of the Shepherd and the *Orans* tend to occupy prime positions on the walls or vaults on which they are frescoed; sometimes, however, their purpose seems to be to connect various iconographic motifs. Decorative themes borrowed from the plant or animal world frequently embellish the images of the Shepherd and the *Orans* and help create a restful atmosphere denoting peace and comfort and alluding clearly to the Resurrection and eternal life. Roman catacomb art was not intended to provoke feelings of sadness and distress.

In terms of iconographical analysis, the Shepherd alludes to Christ while the *Orans* alludes to the Christian who has been saved. Taken together, the figures of the Shepherd and the *Orans* 'clearly suggest the two poles of the act of salvation' (Bisconti), intended to generate in the observer a feeling of trustful waiting for the Resurrection, which will be obtained through Christ. During the third and fourth centuries, the relationship between Christian art and the Bible became even stronger: an ever-increasing number of scenes inspired by characters or episodes from the Old Testament and the New Testament began to appear on the walls of galleries, on the vaults of the *cubicula*, or burial chambers, and, later, on the sarcophagi. For the most part, these biblical subjects were selected and appropriated for their

Figure 1: *Shepherd and Orantes: Scenes from the Jonah Cycle.*
Catacomb of Saints Petrus and Marcellinus, Rome, *cubiculum* 51, vault.
© Foto Pontificia Commissione di Archeologia Sacra, Rome.

sacramental significance: for example, the baptismal or eucharistic iconography connected with texts relating the Baptism of Christ (Matthew 3.13–17; Mark 1.9–11; Luke 3.21–22) or to the Eucharist (Matthew 26.26–29; Mark 14.22–25; Luke 22.14–20; 1 Corinthians 11.23–26). The baptismal scenes tend to feature the Baptism of Christ rather than that of some anonymous worshipper, as evidenced by the almost ever-present image of the dove: this symbolizes the Holy Spirit, which according to the Gospel stories (Matthew 3.16; Mark 1.10; Luke 3.22) came down upon Jesus in the guise of a dove during his Baptism. The most common iconographic representation shows the baptized figure half-immersed in a stream of water, his arms by his sides; in front of him is another male figure, shown in the solemn gesture of the imposition of hands (*impositio manuum*). The eucharistic theme, which runs right through Christian art from its origins, is expressed by the simple imagery of bread and wine or, more often, it is suggested by paintings of banqueting scenes, sometimes generalized and sometimes alluding specifically to the narrative of the Marriage at Cana (John 2.1–11). Scholars have recognized more than one semantic level in the banqueting scenes: in addition to the Eucharist for instance, they can also be connected to the Christian habit of holding funeral banquets (known as *refrigeria*).

The presence of this iconographical tradition in the Roman catacombs confirms that Baptism and the Eucharist were already central to the life of the Christian communities between the second and third centuries. The importance of these sacramental acts is also confirmed by the earliest literary sources. Baptism is referred to in works such as the *Didache* and Justin's *Apologia*. The *Didache*, which can be dated to the end of the first century CE and was aimed largely at Christians emerging from paganism, is an anonymous compilation of sources linked with traditions of various Christian communities. Justin, although he was born in Samaria (Sichem, now Nablus), lived and taught in Rome in the second century CE: he must therefore have been well acquainted with the liturgical and sacramental practices of that particular community. References to the sacrament of the Eucharist can be found in the *Didache* (9–10) and in Justin's *Apologia* (65–67) as well as in some of the Epistles of St Ignatius of Antioch (*Ephesians* 20,2; *Philadelphians* 4; *Smyrnaeans* 7,1), which can be dated to the early second century, and in Pliny the Younger's Epistle to Trajan (*ep.* 10. 96, 7), during the former's tenure as Imperial Governor of Bithynia from 111 to 113. Besides these works and authors, there are others that are equally important with regard to establishing parallels with Early Christian art: I refer to the writings of the so-called Clemens Romanus, who lived in the time of the apostles, and the work known as *The Shepherd of Erma*, both dated to the end of the first or early second century CE. For example, by analysing the

contents of the Third Vision of *The Shepherd of Erma*, which focuses
on a tower as a symbol of the Church, scholars have deciphered the
true meaning of a fresco in the Catacomb of San Gennaro in Naples.
Previously, the painting, which shows a group of people near a tower,
had been traditionally interpreted as being an allusion to the Tower of
Babel (Genesis 11.1–9) but the portrayal of this episode from the Bible
would have been a unique instance in Early Christian iconography.
This example illustrates how aspects of Early Christian art and literature can shed light on each other and thus help clarify obscurities in
both.

Other subjects of particular interest in the Early Christian iconographical repertory are: Adam and Eve (Genesis 2–3), Noah and the
Ark (Genesis 7–8), Moses striking the rock (Exodus 17.1–7), Daniel
in the lions' den (Daniel 6.11–25; 14.31–42), the three young Jews of
Babylon in the fiery furnace (Daniel 3), the story of Susanna (Daniel
13.1–64), the healing of the paralytic (Matthew 9.1–8; Mark 2.1–12;
Luke 5.18–26) and Lazarus brought back from the dead (John
11.1–44). All these, like other biblical themes, are depicted by means
of attributes that have to be decoded and interpreted both in relation
to the biblical text and to the funerary context in question.

The portrayal of Adam and Eve involves a varied iconographic
typology, often articulated in a narrative cycle comprising a series of
scenes that include Creation, Fall and Expulsion from the Garden of
Eden. The story of Noah is synthesized, depicting a half-length male
with arms outstretched leaning out from the Ark; the scene often also
includes a bird carrying a sprig in its beak, which is an obvious
allusion to the narrative of Genesis 8.6–12. The biblical story relates
that, after the forty days of the deluge, Noah sent the birds (first a
raven and then a dove) on different occasions out of the Ark until the
dove returned with a sprig of olive. The fourth time, when the dove
failed to return, Noah understood that the flood waters had subsided
for good. The iconography of the bird therefore signifies the moment
at which the salvation of those in the Ark had been secured: in Noah's

case, the salvation attained is also expressed through the symbol and attitude of his outstretched arms.

Iconographic scenes depicting Moses are extremely frequent in early Christian art; the patriarch is usually characterized by the attribute of the rod (*virga salutis*), either pointing towards or striking the rock, causing water to spring forth. The story of Jonah is often depicted in a narrative cycle in which the prophet is shown being thrown into the sea by the sailors and swallowed by a marine monster of serpentine form, then escaping from the monster's mouth, and finally lying beneath a pergola hung with a type of vegetable that resemble courgettes or little pumpkins. On which biblical text did the artists rely? The Vulgate of St Jerome, the fifth-century Latin translation of the Bible, actually specifies *hedera* (ivy) as being the plant that God caused to grow above the prophet in order to give him shade and refreshment (Jonah 4.6). In a note to this text, moreover, St Jerome points out that he deliberately changed the name of the plant from the original Hebrew because it was the name of an arboreal species unknown in the West. In the Hebrew text, however, the term (*qîqayôn*) is used which the Greek Septuagint translation interpreted as *kolokuntha* and the Vetus Latina version as *cucurbita*: in all three cases the word alludes to a vegetable similar to a pumpkin. Christian art thus clearly takes its inspiration from the earlier Old Testament Latin translation rather than from the Vulgate, which is hardly surprising, bearing in mind the fact that Christian iconography came into being well before St Jerome's version. In any event, the scene depicting Jonah beneath the pergola is intended to portray the moment at which the prophet, having completed his mission with the Ninevites, has acquired salvation; this event in other scenes, as discussed above, is shown by the attitude of outstretched arms (*expansis manibus*) of the persons concerned (Noah, Susanna, Daniel in the lions' den, the three Jews of Babylon, etc.). In some cases the four stages in the cycle of Jonah are reduced to a single narrative but it is the last scene (Jonah beneath the pergola) which is, of course, the most important (Figure 2).

Figure 2: *Jonah's Rest*. Catacomb of Saints Petrus and Marcellinus, Rome, *cubiculum* 67, vault.
© Foto Pontificia Commissione di Archeologia Sacra, Rome.

The Book of Daniel was also a major source of inspiration for Early Christian artists; the earliest catacomb paintings (in the catacomb of Domitilla and the Crypt of Lucina at Callixtus) show the prophet as a praying figure (*orans*) with two animal figures at his feet. The Jewish brothers Ananias, Azaria and Mishael are characterized by their oriental-style headgear and they too are shown as *orantes*, surrounded by tongues of flame. Susanna is also shown with outstretched arms (*expansis manibus*), sometimes with an open book in her hands; her story is often pictured, like those of Adam and Eve and Jonah, in a narrative cycle.

The New Testament tales of healing, given their obvious importance, appeared at an early stage in Christian cemeterial art (the catacomb of Domitilla; the Greek Chapel in the catacomb of Priscilla;

Cubiculum of the Sacraments in the catacomb of Callixtus). The iconography of the episode concerning the paralytic varies, but it is nevertheless characterized by the attribute of the bed which he usually carries on his back. The story of Lazarus is depicted by the portrayal of a person swathed in bandages, standing at the entrance to a small temple or sort of aedicule that represents the sepulchre; the figure of Christ is shown next to him touching his head with the rod (*virga*). In Early Christian art, the rod was an attribute of both Moses and Christ: this is due to the fact that the Christians saw Moses as being a prefiguration of Christ. This interpretation is widely documented, both in art and in exegetical literature. The rod is the attribute with which Christ works miracles on the deceased or on inanimate objects, whereas in the case of living persons, the miracle is represented by the outstretched hand of the Saviour.

From a stylistic point of view, the Early Christian artists used an extremely synthetic and symbolic figurative vocabulary. The narrative nucleus of the episodes from the Bible, as previously noted, was pared down to the essential so that the paintings focused on one or two figures associated with characteristic signs and attributes. Furthermore, the scenes tended to be on a small scale since in the catacombs the spaces for the wall decorations were provided by continuous lines that made up quite small geometrical sections.

From the time of Constantine (274–337) onwards, Christian art began to encompass other subjects: the inclusion of new scenes from the Bible reflects the rapid spread of Christianity and the accompanying mass conversions that brought large numbers of new worshippers into the existing communities. Such new worshippers were probably less strongly motivated and possessed only a rudimentary knowledge of the Bible. This led to the need for encouraging a more extensive and comprehensive knowledge of the Bible, a need which was met in various ways: on an artistic level through iconography; through the spoken word by means of the homily; in literature with the steady dissemination of biblical exegesis not only in the East, but also in the

West. Consequently, we can assume that one of the main aims of Christian art was now strongly didactic, even though there continues to be a lively debate on this issue. If we admit that the didactic function of Christian art was an important one, though perhaps not the principal one, we must also acknowledge that the faithful must have had enough biblical background to be able to recognize, at the very least, the frescoed scenes, although their extreme graphic succinctness could render them hard to identify. Much of the average worshipper's biblical knowledge was probably only of a general nature: it is unlikely that the public would have had a direct acquaintance with reading the Scriptures – as opposed to hearing them read aloud during liturgical celebrations. We must presume that there were several levels at which the scenes could be read, ranging from simple recognition of the subjects to a perception of their theological content, and the personal elaboration of new concepts on the basis of the images depicted.

Early Christian art and its biblical background

Why did Early Christian art concentrate on depicting some biblical subjects rather than others? In order to understand the reasons, both the location and the historical circumstances in which Christian art developed must be taken into consideration. In terms of location, it is natural that Christians should have wanted to use visual images as a means of expressing a consoling message within a sepulchral setting, as the texts of many epigraphs also demonstrate. Christian funerary inscriptions, from the third century onwards, lay emphasis on the deceased's passing on to a better life. The concept of the soul passing to God and the body resting while waiting for the final Resurrection was central. This explains why the paintings are influenced by soteriological motifs and promote either the idea of eternal salvation or the sacramental means by which this can be achieved. All the Old and

New Testament stories that were expressed visually were those that could be interpreted as paradigms of salvation: by engaging with biblical visual images, the worshipper – whatever his or her social conditions, level of doctrinal knowledge or biblical understanding – would learn that Christ would save his followers in the same way that the shepherd brings the lost sheep safely home. The viewer was also encouraged to identify with the way Noah is saved from the flood (Figure 3), Jonah pulled from the whale, Daniel rescued from the lions, the three young Jews saved from the fiery furnace, Susanna plucked from the clutches of the lustful elderly judges, the paralytic healed and Lazarus brought back to life. To a certain extent, an observer's identification of the characters in the paintings would have had to be intuitive, just as the perception of the Christological value of them.

Scholars have noted a subtle difference in the way episodes from the Old Testament and the New Testament are portrayed. In the case of New Testament episodes, their salvific message comes across explicitly in the visual narrative itself, since healing or sacramental scenes were appropriate vehicles to portray messages of physical and spiritual redemption. The salvific value of Old Testament subjects, on the other hand, is mediated through the New Testament or exegetical literature which affirms their importance through symbolic or Christological interpretation. While the New Testament episodes played a predominantly narrative function, the Old Testament episodes had a more markedly symbolic function. The tendency to favour those Old Testament subjects confirmed in the New Testament and to portray both Old and New Testament characters and episodes in the same *cubiculum* (and often on the same wall) was evidently intended to place the Old and New Laws on the same line of the history of salvation – for reasons that were probably not only anti-Jewish but also anti-Gnostic. In Rome, during the second century, doctrines abounded (such as that professed by Marcion) that undermined the authority of the Old Testament and the God of the Old Testament, giving

Figure 3: *Noah and his Ark*. Catacomb of Saints Petrus and Marcellinus, Rome, *cubiculum* 64, entrance wall.
© Foto Pontificia Commissione di Archeologia Sacra, Rome.

precedence to the New Testament and the God of the New Testament. The latter was seen as a quite distinct and superior entity to the Old Testament divinity. It is exactly because of its opposition to doctrines of this kind that the official Church firmly insisted on the continuity between the Old and New Testaments and used the medium of iconography as one of the most important and effective ways of getting its message across.

Regarding the historical background to the development of Christian art, it should be kept in mind that the hostilities between the Roman Empire and Christianity were at their height during the third century: for example, the persecutions of Decius (251), Valerianus (257–8) and, above all, Diocletian (301–12). The importance of these events has often been exaggerated in apologetic historiography; however, there is no doubt that adherents to the Christian faith during these years ran a real risk of possible martyrdom. Christianity actually remained an illegal religion until 313, when the Emperor Constantine met Licinius in Milan and issued his Edict of Toleration. The search for paradigmatic models of salvation in Paleo-Christian art seems, therefore, to reflect the climate of danger and uncertainty surrounding the earliest Christians. The historical circumstances and the need for Christians to conceal their faith because they lived in a hostile environment may well have contributed to the emphasis on symbolism discernible in the iconographic and epigraphic output of the time. The use of the fish as a Christological symbol dates from this era, for example. It is well known that the Greek term for fish (*Ichthus*) makes up the acronym for the phrase *Iesous Christos Theou Uios Soter* (Jesus Christ, Son of God, Saviour): it is a real, albeit succinct, profession of faith.

The inspiration provided by the Bible is of the utmost significance for an appreciation of the nature of Early Christian art. It is important to appreciate the role played by the Bible for Christians during the first few centuries and the difference in perception between the Old and New Testaments. The Old Testament was the sacred Scripture that Christians shared with Jews; as such, it constituted a serious source of disagreement between these two religious communities. Right from the beginning, in fact, Christian literature attests to conflict between the Christians and the Jews on the value of the Old Testament, which often took the form of polemic writings. In essence, the Christians reclaimed the covenant made by JHWH with Israel for themselves, also claiming the right and the ability to interpret the entire Old Testament in a Christological vein. From an early Christian perspective, the characters and episodes from the history of Israel contained in the Old Testament would all have been intended to prefigure Christ and the Christian message. The relationship with the Old Testament in primitive Christianity was further complicated, as has been alluded to, by the existence of schools of thought that discredited the authority of this early part of Scripture: for example, Marcion. Obviously there were no difficulties of this kind with the New Testament, which was regarded as an exclusively Christian Scripture. However, the fact that the New Testament canon was only definitively established in the early sixth century may have caused something of a problem: not all the texts that the Christians originally held to be inspired were later accepted by the canon.

Clearly, within this context, Christians were extremely keen to stress the continuity and harmony that existed between the Old and New Testaments, both interpreted, albeit differently, in the light of Christ. This message was passed on to the faithful through all available channels: through preaching, literature and art. In literature, from the second century onwards, biblical exegesis emphasizing the Christological role of numerous Old Testament characters and interpreting the history of Israel in a Christological key was promoted (for example, all the episodes involving water became baptismal symbols). However, it would be wrong to place too much emphasis on the literature that the faithful had access to, since in Late Antiquity only a cultured and wealthy elite were able to read. Apart from the difficulties posed by the inability of many worshippers to get to grips with a written text, there was the added problem of the availability of books (including the Bible): it therefore follows that biblical knowledge and Christian doctrine were essentially passed on by word of mouth. This is hardly surprising bearing in mind the fact that Christian instruction was given through prayer, catechism and homilies. Art, too, had its place along with the catechism and other instruments of oral communication for the propagation of biblical and Christian knowledge. Various iconographical paradigms came into existence in order to convey a doctrine or theology that had already been established; iconography provided the means by which that doctrine could reach a much wider audience.

Conclusion

Recognizing and being able to define precisely the criteria according to which a figure or a biblical episode was accepted into the pictorial or sculptural repertory is clearly of tremendous importance. Summarizing the criteria already indicated, we should emphasize first the desire to reassert the continuity of the Old and New Testaments in a salvific perspective. Second, as we have also seen, we must recognize the great emphasis placed on Baptism and the Eucharist, sacraments that can be directly connected to the New Testament writings. Last but not least, we need to concentrate on identifying the sources from which the iconographers and their patrons drew each individual theme. In order to do this, we need to find out what kind of biblical education the Early Christian communities had. Are we to believe that they were only familiar with the stories handed down through the canonical Scriptures? Some details of certain iconographical subjects would lead us to believe otherwise, and this hypothesis is reinforced by the fact that, even in many Christian literary texts, there are elements that derive from extra-canonical narratives. This should come as no surprise bearing in mind the fact that, for the reasons set out above, reading directly from the Bible could not have been a wide-spread activity. The characters and episodes that reflected the biblical culture of Christian communities must therefore – as we have seen – have been encountered through stories told aloud that were associated with each other to varying degrees. For instance, two different types of iconography can be identified for Job: the first, an older version, shows him as a male figure sitting, in a reflective frame of mind; the second, which only became widespread during the mid fourth century, includes the presence of at least one female figure next to Job, identifiable as his wife, portrayed in the act of holding something out to him on a staff or stick. The typology of Job with his wife is predominantly attested to on sarcophagi and in some catacombs; there is an example of it, as we have seen, in the private 'anonymous catacomb' of the Via Latina. The iconographic scheme of the woman with a staff is indecipherable if interpreted only in the light of the canonical Book of Job: in order to understand the details, one must refer to the extra-canonical version, the so-called Testament of Job, dated to between the first century BCE and the first century CE. A second example is the Nativity: it is worth bearing in mind that much iconography associated with the Nativity provides for the presence of the ox and the ass beside Mary and the child. This has been traced back to various Old Testament texts (for example, Isaiah 1.3), but there is no mention of them in the New Testament canonical texts, although they are referred to in the Gospel of Pseudo-Matthew. The earliest surviving image of the Nativity is interesting. The fresco of the Virgin Mary in the central area of the Catacomb of Priscilla, painted in around 230 CE, shows a male figure pointing to a star as well as the female figure with the child in her arms. This is probably an Old Testament character, whose identity has long been a subject for discussion (Isaiah? Balaam? David?): in any case the painting was intended, through the presence of an Old Testament figure, to provide a response to those, be they Jews or Gnostics, who denied the unity of the Old and New Testaments and cast doubts on the divinity of Christ.

It is worth repeating that, when studying a figurative Early Christian work of art, not only must its formal aspects be taken careful note of, but also its context – almost always an archaeological context – and its value as a tangible and concrete expression of the Christian community to which it belongs. In particular, when assessing the relationship between Christian art and the Bible, it should be stressed that this relationship cannot be confined merely to those biblical books now deemed to be canonical. On the contrary, we now believe that extra-canonical literature had a strong influence on early Christianity, as evidenced by its general manifestations among the faithful, in the exegesis of the church Fathers and, most significantly, in art. It is my belief that taking these factors into account when analysing depictions of biblical characters in early Christian art could well provide scholars with important evaluative tools and open up new avenues of research.

Note

1   The case of Dura Europos is worthy of note. Sited on the River Euphrates, this Syrian city was destroyed by the Parthians in 256. As well as a Jewish synagogue, there was also a *domus ecclesia* that was used by the Christians for baptismal purposes. Both these buildings were frescoed, and the date when the site was destroyed provides us with a definite latest date for the paintings. The iconographical repertory attested to at Dura Europos is often very similar to the iconographical repertory of the Roman catacombs.

Suggested reading

F. Bisconti, *Temi di iconografia paleocristiana* (Vatican City: Pontificio Istituto di Archeologia, 2000).

V. Fiocchi Nicolai, F. Bisconti and D. Mazzoleni, *Le catacombe cristiane di*

Roma. Origini, sviluppo, apparati decorativi, documentazione epigrafica (Regensburg: Schnell & Steiner Verlag, 1998).

A. Grabar, *Christian Iconography: A Study of Its Origin* (Princeton: Princeton University Press, 1968).

3

The Bible and medieval art

JOHN MORGAN-GUY

Biblical imagery was so important in medieval times that most art from this period is indecipherable without constant reference to the Bible. A second important aspect is patronage and a third is the medieval concept of time, unfamiliar perhaps to our present age. John Morgan-Guy presents an overview of the importance of the Bible in medieval art and reflects on some of the many questions it poses.

Introduction

'Medieval' as a concept is difficult to define. When in 1849 J. H. Parker published the first edition of his *An Introduction to Gothic Architecture* – building styles and construction techniques inextricably bound up with notions of the 'medieval' – he felt it necessary to begin with the architecture of the Romans, and carried his survey forward to 1547 and the death of Henry VIII. There remain good grounds, 150 years later, for understanding 'medieval' as a term which can embrace so wide an expanse of the recorded history of Western civilization. For the purposes of this chapter, the definition has been drawn rather tighter; from the emergence of Romanesque art and architecture, which many scholars see as the first truly 'international' style, during the tenth to twelfth centuries, through to the major upheavals in the religious thought and practice of Western Europe in the mid sixteenth century which are familiarly known as the Reformation.

'All art properly so called is religious, because all art properly so called is an affirmation of absolute values.' That was the understanding of the sculptor Eric Gill (1882–1940), and at no time in history was that understanding more true than during the Middle Ages, the period that has been called the 'high summer of the creative imagination'. This was the time when, in the sculptor Edward Robinson's words – he was writing in 1993 – there existed

> an awareness that there was nothing in heaven and earth that did not, or could not, reflect the glory of its divine creator, nothing that could not have its place in the worship of a God who had made humanity in his own likeness.[1]

Distinctions between 'sacred' and 'secular' were all but meaningless. Medieval art is religious art, what Robinson called 'the door by which the holy is to be approached, to be celebrated, to be worshipped'. It has the intention and the potential to evoke reverence, to intensify faith, and, because so much of it was inspired by biblical narrative, to deepen and enrich the understanding of the text. It is not, however, just illustrative of the text, or a commentary upon it; rather, it needs to be seen as a Bible in its own right, a sacred Scripture which has come down to us in parallel to the written word.

Some questions posed by medieval biblical art

High on the north wall of the chancel of the church of St Mary de Crypt in Gloucester can be seen the greater part of a mural painting executed some time early in the sixteenth century. The subject is the Adoration of the Magi (Matthew 2.11). The artist is unknown, but on stylistic grounds is thought to have been Flemish. The painting, in oils directly onto the wall, was hidden from view for more years than it was visible. Possibly within 20 years of its completion it was covered with lime-wash, and it was only rediscovered in 1842, along with a far more fragmentary but complementary work by the same artist on the south wall.

This Gloucester mural helps to direct our attention to a number of the questions posed by medieval art-work. When was it created and by whom? Who paid for it? What message or messages is the artist conveying and to whom? Trying to answer at least some of these questions will introduce us to the main themes of this chapter. Further, both the mural's damaged condition and its history are timely reminders of how much art-work of this period has been lost to us through sometimes violent religious change, and also simply through neglect, changing fashion and the passage of time.

It is by no means easy to date precisely such a work of art as this, but all the evidence would point to the first quarter of the sixteenth century. Does this provide any clue as to a possible patron? Although the painting is in the chancel, the repair and upkeep of which was the responsibility of the rector (from the twelfth century, the prior and community of Lanthony Secunda), it is unlikely that the work was undertaken at the priory's expense. By 1518 the community was short of money and unable to repair its own buildings properly. So a likely patron should be sought from among the leading citizens of Gloucester at that time – that is, from among the merchants, especially those known to be closely associated with this particular church. There would seem to be two obvious candidates.

The first is John Cooke, one of the first aldermen of the city under Richard III's new charter for the city in 1483, four times mayor, and by the time of his death in 1528 by far the wealthiest man in Gloucester. He and his wife Joan, who outlived him by nearly 20 years, were generous benefactors of the churches in the city, but especially of St Mary de Crypt, where they were buried, and where their memorial brasses still survive. John Cooke was described as a 'mercer', a dealer in woollen and linen goods, and that trade would have brought him in contact with businessmen in Bristol, London and probably on the continent as well. Cooke was one of the few men in the city – probably fewer than a dozen in all – who would have had sufficient personal wealth to finance such a decorative scheme as the one that survives in St Mary de Crypt.

Another and more shadowy candidate, who in his will of 1506 left money and property to the church to found a chantry (as well as vestments and plate for its service), was Garet van Eck, whose name might indicate that he was of Flemish origin. This may be significant, as van Eck almost certainly maintained trading and probably familial links with his homeland, and, as noted above, the style of the murals would indicate a Flemish artist. When the paintings were conserved in 1982, the restorers were fairly confident of this attribution, and could not think of an English artist who was equipped to have undertaken the work in this way.

We shall probably never know for certain, but one or other of these men, if not both, is the most likely patron. There is one clue that it may indeed have been a collaborative effort between Cooke and van Eck. In the painting of the Adoration of the Magi, in the gallery depicted above the head of the Blessed Virgin Mary there appear two male figures in contemporary dress, looking down on the scene, with one pointing to it. Portraits of donors are a commonplace in works of this kind, and it is not impossible that these two men represent Cooke and van Eck. Certainly later on, after their deaths, they seem to have shared a chantry altar, and this may suggest that they had been associated in life as well as in death. This concern with the identity of the donor or donors is vitally important for the subject of medieval art. It is a reminder that, without patronage and religious impulse, very little of the art of this period would have been created. Patrons were important, and they had much to say over the choice of subject matter.

The Adoration of the Magi was one such popular subject. The 'three Kings' were adopted as patrons and protectors by travellers and pilgrims alike, and would certainly have been popular with those, like the Gloucester merchants, whose livelihood depended upon sometimes long and hazardous trading journeys. This mural, with the Magi in the rich costume of the early sixteenth century and the contemporary onlookers of the scene, is a reminder of the immediacy of the biblical text for its creators, patrons and artist alike. Past, present and future were not for them simply concepts in linear time; they were inextricable, what has been called 'depth dimensions within each other'.

Art, suffering and healing

A generation or so before the Gloucester mural was painted, another work of art arrived in England, to find its home in a rather different ecclesiastical setting. The Almshouse of St John the Baptist and St John the Evangelist at Sherborne in Dorset was founded in 1437 by the bishop of Salisbury with the support of King Henry VI. Structurally it has the form of a church, with the chancel and altar (consecrated in 1442) forming the focal point, and the nave, in two storeys, as the accommodation for the residents. The community of 'twelve pore feeble and ympotent old men and four old women', cared for by a matron and a chaplain, were required to 'hear one messe' daily, and five times daily to recite 'our Lady sauter'. Prayer and worship were therefore at the heart of this as of every community.

About 50 years after its foundation, as a gift, the chapel altar was adorned with a new reredos in the form of a triptych (Figure 4). As with the Gloucester murals, both artist and donor remain unknown, though on stylistic grounds a date of about 1480 is normally given to the painting and it is generally accepted as being of Flemish workmanship. Again, as with the Gloucester murals, it was probably forgotten for more years than it was on view. The upheavals of the Reformation era saw it banished to an obscure corner, where it lay ignored and in bad repair, the wings of the triptych closed up, until at least the nineteenth century.

Figure 4: *The Sherborne Triptych.*
© The Master and Brethren of the Almshouse of St John the Baptist and
St John the Evangelist, Sherborne, and The Victoria and Albert Museum, London.

The subject matter is entirely appropriate for a hospital or almshouse. At Sherborne the central panel depicts the raising of Lazarus
(John 11.1–46). An emaciated figure of Lazarus emerging from his
grave occupies the centre foreground. To the left are grouped the figures
of Christ – a serene but authoritative depiction – with Mary Magdalene
and the apostles. The representation of the Magdalene is striking; she is
shown in the left foreground, easily identifiable by her long, flowing
hair, but with her head turned away, as if overwhelmed by what she is
witnessing. Two of the apostles – the only two whose faces are clearly
delineated – turn to look compassionately at her. Finding Martha in the
scene is more problematic. Is she the richly garbed woman (alone in the
left-hand group portrayed without a halo) standing on Jesus's left? Or
is she the equally richly dressed woman in the right foreground, leaning
towards Lazarus, her hands clasped in prayer? And who is the kneeling
man behind Lazarus and supporting him with his hands whose features
might indicate a portrait? Indeed, are the man and the woman shown
so prominently in close proximity to Lazarus the donors of the painting
to the almshouse?

To their right is a group of men and women whose expressions reveal degrees of scepticism and wonder, no doubt those referred to by John in 11.36–37. One of them, leaning on a spade, is clearly the gravedigger. In the background is a walled and castellated town, representing Bethany, and above all within a circle of cloud and light is the triple-crowned figure of God the Father, his right hand raised in blessing. Each wing of the triptych depicts two further miracles of Jesus, in the form of a main and a subsidiary picture. On the left the principal image is that of the casting out of a demon (Luke 11.14–20 and Matthew 9.32–34) and on the right the raising to life of the son of the widow of Nain (Luke 7.11–16). The subsidiary inset panels depict the restoration of sight to Bartimaeus the son of Timaeus (Mark 10.46–52) and the raising of Jairus' daughter (Mark 5.22–43 and Luke 8.41–56).

These subjects, drawn from all four Gospels, have been very carefully chosen for this altarpiece, emphasizing as they do the healing and revivifying power of Jesus. All are bound together (implicitly, for the text is nowhere spelled out) by Jesus's affirmation to Martha 'I am the resurrection and the life: he that believeth in me, though he were dead, yet shall he live: and whosoever liveth and believeth in me shall never die' (John 11.25–26). The altarpiece was intended as a comfort and consolation to the aged sick and afflicted who prayed daily before it, just as much as the written text was intended to be for those who read and meditated upon it.

It is impossible not to draw a parallel with the famous Isenheim altarpiece, now in the Unterlinden Museum in Alsace and dating from perhaps 30 years later than the Sherborne triptych. Matthias Grünewald (c. 1460–1528) in this striking and most moving work was, like the anonymous Sherborne artist, providing a focus for the devotion of the sick and the disabled. We know that at Isenheim the sick were carried to the foot of the altar to participate in the liturgy, and the sacramental presence of Christ in the Mass, allied with the vivid and uncompromising depiction of his suffering during crucifixion, combined to reinforce faith, to kindle hope of resurrection if not of healing in this life, and to assure the sufferers and bring them the understanding that even in the worst of their affliction they were not denied the love of God.

As with the Gloucester murals, the question of the donor or donors remains unresolved in the case of the Sherborne altarpiece. Several figures appear in late fifteenth-century dress in the panels, any one of which could be a donor portrait. It could be the man in the left-hand panel, wearing a sword indicative of his rank, here shown holding up the staggering, deranged figure of the demoniac and bringing him to Jesus. It could be the ecclesiastic, or, as suggested above, the man and woman supporting and praying for Lazarus in the central panel. The likely explanation is that the cost of this splendid altarpiece was borne by a wealthy and well-connected Dorset family.

Knowing the artist

Sometimes, perhaps surprisingly frequently, it is possible to answer the questions that have concerned us so far; who was the artist, and who paid for the work? Contrary to widespread opinion, the identity of the artist of a particular work can on occasion be established on other than stylistic grounds. Sometimes the work is signed. Artists' signatures do survive even from the Romanesque period (eleventh to twelfth century), though this is more common in mainland Europe than it is in England. Two examples of identifiable artists would be Gislebertus, a sculptor working at Autun Cathedral c. 1130 (see Figure 5), and Gerlachus, a glass-painter at the Premonstratensian Arnstein abbey near Coblenz on the Rhine some 20 years later.

Gislebertus is justly celebrated, not the least for his figure of Eve, now in the Musée Rolin at Autun but formerly in the cathedral. The figure of a horizontal, languorous, naked Eve, reaching behind her for an apple, has been described as one of the most erotically charged images of Romanesque art. (Gislebertus may also have been

Figure 5: Gislebertus, *Eve* (c. 1130). Autun, Musée Rolin.
Photograph: Stéphane Prost.

responsible for the capital from St Etienne Cathedral, Toulouse, depicting Salome receiving the head of John the Baptist and dancing before Herod as narrated in Matthew 14.6–11. Here again the artist conveys an atmosphere of allure and lust.) Gerlachus, on the other hand, simply puts himself in the picture. A stained-glass panel, c. 1150, now in the Westphalian State Museum of Art and Cultural History at Münster, gives us a portrait of the artist, brush in one hand and paint-pot in the other. It is believed that he was the donor of the window in which he appears.

An excellent example of our knowledge of artist and donor, and one contemporary with the Sherborne triptych, is the Dwnn altarpiece, now in the National Gallery in London. Sir John Dwnn of Cydweli in south-west Wales was a close and trusted counsellor of King Edward IV, who employed him on a number of delicate embassies to the courts of France and Burgundy. Like his patron he was a notable collector of rich and costly illuminated manuscripts, at least two of which contain his portrait. Most importantly, however, in 1478 or 1479 he commissioned Hans Memling of Bruges to paint an altarpiece, a triptych probably intended for a domestic chapel in his home in Calais. Memling (c. 1440–94) was then one of the most celebrated and accomplished artists working in the Low Countries, and the Dwnn altarpiece is comparable with his *The Mystic Marriage of St Catherine*, which he completed in the same year.

The centre panel of the Dwnn altarpiece shows the Virgin Mary, seated in a loggia with a book and the Christ-child on her lap. To her right kneels Sir John Dwnn, and to her left his wife Elizabeth and their daughter. Behind Sir John stands the figure of St Catherine, and behind Lady Elizabeth St Barbara. The two wings of the triptych contain the figures of Sir John's patron saints, John the Baptist and John the Evangelist. In the left-hand panel, lurking behind a pillar, is an unidentified male figure thought by some including Germain Bazin, a commentator on Memling, to be the artist himself. (In this respect Memling would be standing in the tradition of Gerlachus, and, interestingly, the restorers of the St Mary de Crypt mural tentatively identified one figure now largely destroyed as a self-portrait of the anonymous artist.)

Memling, in common with many other medieval artists, frequently included portraits of the donors in his work, and the reason for this was not solely because they were holding the purse-strings. The evidence of other surviving portraits of Dwnn makes it quite clear that Memling's is taken from life. (Resident as he was from time to time at the Burgundian ducal court, Dwnn would have been available for sittings.) Another very good example, perhaps ten years later than the Dwnn altarpiece, is the diptych of Martin van Nieuvenhove, now at St John's Hospital in Bruges. It is a work packed with theological allusions. The diptych includes an outstanding portrait of Martin, and behind him, set into the window, is a representation of St Martin of Tours dividing his cloak for a beggar. It is the incident in the early life of the fourth-century saint for which he is best remembered and here it not only recalls the donor's patron saint but also, for those who did not know, indicates that his name was Martin.

In the other panel of the Nieuvenhove diptych Memling shows the Blessed Virgin Mary with the Christ-child. Mary is painted holding an apple, and the child reaches out for it. This is not just a charming composition. Mary is the second Eve, whose purity and obedience through her submission to her God-given vocation (Luke 1.26–38) gives to humankind the Person and means by which the consequences of the disobedience of the first Eve are reversed. By tradition, the forbidden fruit which Eve, at the prompting of the serpent, took, ate and gave to Adam, was the apple (Genesis 3.1–7). Here that same fruit, of the tree of the knowledge of good and evil (Genesis 2.17), can be taken in the fullness of innocence, by Christ, as he is himself 'the way, the truth, and the life' (John 14.6). A theological message, ultimately deriving from the biblical narrative, is thus included by the artist in his composition. In such a way, the visual biblical narrative, a 'parallel' text, fills out and illuminates the understanding of the written text.

Over and over again in medieval art we find the biblical narrative and theological exegesis at the heart of the composition. It is not an exaggeration to say that medieval art was soaked in scriptural reference. To return to Autun Cathedral and the work of Gislebertus in the twelfth century: in another example of his work we find the artist focusing upon the story of the Magi from Matthew 2. One capital depicts Matthew 2.13, the warning dream they shared which sent them back not to Herod, but 'into their own country another way'. Gislebertus' composition here is one of the most delightful of his works. He has shown the three Magi as kings, in one bed and under a blanket, identified by the crowns that they still wear in their sleep. Over them hovers the angel, pointing with one hand to the star which has been their guiding light (Matthew 2.2, 9–10). With his finger, the angel very gently touches the hand of one of the kings, and thus awakens him – a moment brilliantly shown by the open eyes and rather startled and bemused expression of the king. This capital was rightly described by a former bishop of Oxford, Dr Richard Harries, as a sermon in stone, the message of which he drew out very well in his *A Gallery of Reflections: The Nativity of Christ* (Lion, 1995). God does not abandon any of his children, and in caring for them he guides them. The Magi have been brought to Christ; now they are to be seen safely home. The inference in Gislebertus' carving is that the star which they had followed to Bethlehem will also be their guiding light on their long return journey. (The outward journey had taken two years, according to Matthew 2.16.) Bishop Harries also drew attention to the gentle, awakening touch of the angel, which Gislebertus so wonderfully conveys, and draws out its implication. 'The guidance of God is rarely loud and overwhelming. It is usually the slightest touch, the nudge, the hint.'

Expression and an eye for detail

Laying aside modern understandings of realism or likeness, we can confidently say that medieval artists had a genius for capturing expression. We have found this already in the Gislebertus capital and the Sherborne triptych, separated in time by nearly 400 years. It is worth mentioning several further examples to emphasize this point. Medieval artists had a profound understanding of emotion and character, and were able skilfully to reveal both, sometimes with quite remarkable economy. One excellent illustration appears in the St Alban's Psalter of c. 1130, from St Godehard's Church, Hildesheim. One illuminated page depicts Luke 24.10–11, the reaction of the apostles to the announcement of the Lord's Resurrection by the angel at the sepulchre to Mary Magdalene, Joanna and Mary the mother of James. The artist shows only Mary Magdalene and the apostles, but in their expressions of mingled amazement and disbelief, Luke's comment that the women's words 'seemed to them as idle tales, and they believed them not' (v.11) could not be better conveyed. Nor indeed could the Magdalene's rather 'shell-shocked' insistence upon the truth of her message.

Another outstanding example of this genius for expression is to be found in a French verse account of the birth of Jesus, dating from c. 1315–25 and now in the Bodleian Library, Oxford (Plate 3) (MS Selden Supra 38). At the very beginning is an illustration of the Holy Family. The disposition of the figures is conventional. Joseph, to the right, is shown seated and asleep, leaning upon his staff, his expression one of profound weariness. Mary, in the foreground, is shown resting upon a couch, awake, but with an understandable expression of discomfort – the artist's work predates the influential vision of the Nativity of St Bridget of Sweden (1303–73), with its emphasis upon a painless and miraculous birth for Jesus, which was to profoundly affect the iconography of the Nativity in subsequent centuries. But the real focus of attention is the central group of three figures: the Christ-child, the ox and the ass. The swaddled infant lies upon, rather than in, an altar-like manger (itself a 'forward reference' to the sacrifice of Calvary). Only his face is visible, and this bears an expression of watchful anxiety, the eyes turned towards the head of the ass. There is good reason to worry; the ass, his own expression one of sly determination, is in the process of moving aside the clothes which cover the child, his intent clearly to reach the hay filling the manger underneath. Meanwhile the eyes of the ox are turned towards the sleeping Joseph, and the animal's whole expression is one of chuckling amusement. Thus with deft and economic brush-strokes, the artist has brilliantly succeeded in imparting not only great humanity to his depiction of the scene, but also a considerable degree of humour. Once again, the 'parallel' text written by the artist draws out what is, perhaps, only implicit in the written narrative.

A prominent characteristic of the medieval artist was his keen eye for detail, often allied, as in this manuscript illumination, with an economy of line. A further example of this is to be found in another Bodleian Library manuscript (Plate 4) (MS Bodl. 764), which is a mid thirteenth-century Bestiary. This contains an illumination of the three Magi journeying to Bethlehem. They are riding dromedaries, which the artist had clearly never seen – except in other manuscript illustrations or in carvings. In this respect, his depiction is a work of the imagination. But the same cannot be said of the harness, saddles and stirrups. This, right down to bit and bridle, is meticulously portrayed, and the distinctive posture of the three riders shows that the artist, whoever he was, knew how to sit a horse. A similar attention to detail can be found on the twelfth-century stone font in the church of St Mary, Llanfair Clydogau, in Ceredigion, Wales. The bowl of the font is carved with the emblems associated with the four evangelists. All four are confidently cut in bold relief, but, in the case of the emblem of St John the Evangelist, the artist betrays his unfamiliarity with the eagle. The bird here is based upon something more local and familiar, possibly a crow or a raven, or maybe, because of the distinctive curve of the long beak, a seabird or wader. Ceredigion is a county of rivers with a long seaboard. The resulting carving may be a long way from an eagle, but, with a minimum of cutting, the artist has left us with a memorable bird-carving, the fruit of his own observation and experience.

A third and final example of the concern with expression is the late fifteenth-century (c. 1472) central boss in the first bay of the nave of Norwich Cathedral, one of a whole sequence of remarkable bosses in the vaults of that church and of its adjacent cloisters. Boss NA11, as it is designated, depicts the temptation of Adam and Eve by the serpent (Figure 6). It deserves close scrutiny, but, in respect of expression and attention to detail, two things in particular require comment. The first is the expressions on the faces of Eve and Adam. They are in marked contrast; Eve offers Adam the apple, her features composed but with just a hint of apprehension and fear. Adam, receiving the apple, betrays wide-eyed consternation and alarm. The artist has brilliantly captured the moment described in Genesis 3.7, 'and the eyes of them both were opened, and they knew that they were naked'. It is this very nakedness, too, which underlines the artist's attention to detail. He knew his human anatomy. Although in neither figure is there an explicit rendering of genitalia the artist has very carefully shown the difference between the shape of the hips and the swell of the inner thighs that exists in the male and the female, and, although only one breast is shown on the carving of Eve, it is that of a young woman who has not yet suckled an infant. (The configuration is clear, even allowing for what looks like some modern repainting.)

This same roof boss leads us into the consideration of what might be termed the narrative nature of much medieval art. In the Norwich roof boss representing the Fall, there seem at first sight to be four apples. With his left hand the serpent plucks one from the tree; with the right he offers another to Eve. Eve in her turn with her right hand proffers a fruit to Adam, who, in *his* turn clutches a fruit in his left hand to his heart. We have, then, four apples depicted. There is, however, in the artist's intent only one apple. This is his way of indicating the

Figure 6: *Adam, Eve and the Serpent.* Boss NA11, Norwich Cathedral.
© Jarrold Publishing, Norwich.

passage of the forbidden fruit from Satan to Eve and then to Adam. We have here an artistic narrative distillation of Genesis 3.1–6, a narrative, as we saw earlier, which is then completed by the expressions and nakedness of Adam and Eve (3.7). This one boss, a mere 24 inches across, therefore encapsulates the whole of the Fall narrative in one static image. We have already referred to another such narrative carving, Gislebertus' *Dance of Salome*, from St Etienne's Cathedral, Toulouse. Here onto one capital the artist has compressed the whole narrative of Matthew 14.6–11. The Norwich artist and Gislebertus had to meet the challenge of depicting in one static image a narrative which describes actions undertaken sequentially during a passage of time. It is by means of such devices as we have described that they surmounted it.

The depiction of time in medieval art

Works such as these thus pose the important question: if the artist can compress a narrative in this way, what does that tell us about his understanding of time? We can only give an answer if we accept that in the medieval mind the world of the Bible was the real world, what is sometimes called 'the world of the text' – and that text included both pictorial and chirographic: image and writing. From a medieval perspective, there was only one reality and that reality transcended such a concept as the passage of time. Thus the people and the events of the Old Testament were at one and the same time literal – they were within the temporal, historical sequence – and typological. They had their fulfilment in the New Testament. Furthermore, that real world contained within it the response and experience of the reader or viewer at whatever moment in chronological time they lived. Medieval believers saw themselves as part of the narrative and because they did so their own thoughts, actions, passions, the shape of their own lives and that of their community, society and era contributed both literally and typologically to the story because they participated in it. As the writer Arturo Perez-Reverte said of the Flemish artists of the late Middle Ages,

> the sense of realism was so intense that the painting effort-
> lessly achieved the effect sought by the old Flemish masters:
> the integration of the spectator into the pictorial whole,
> persuading him that the space in which he stood was the
> same as that represented in the painting, as if the picture
> were a fragment of reality, or reality a fragment of the
> picture.

One can, in fact, go further than Perez-Reverte, for it was not only the old Flemish masters who achieved this, but medieval artists in general. And it was not just 'as if' the picture were a fragment of reality, it was an expression of that reality. Furthermore, a person's place within this landscape of reality was, as the philosopher Hans Frei recognized, pre-scriptive: that is, people had a duty to fit themselves into that world. By so doing, their own thoughts and actions became in their turn determinative; how they lived their lives and died their deaths within this world of the text mattered in the same way as it had done for Adam, Eve and the saints *with whom and alongside whom they stood.* We are dealing here with what can be called a concept of simultane-ity, where, as we said earlier, reality transcends the spacial and the temporal.

Let us take one final example to illustrate this point, the *Saint Luke Drawing the Virgin* of c. 1435–40 by Rogier van der Weyden (c. 1400–64), now in the Boston Museum of Fine Arts (Figure 7). In this painting the Blessed Virgin Mary is shown in the left foreground, suckling the infant Jesus. In the right foreground, dressed in the robes of a high-ranking ecclesiastic of the fifteenth century, St Luke is shown sketching the Virgin and Child. In the background, seen through the arches of a loggia, appears a Flemish river and townscape, and in the middle distance a man and a woman stand looking out from a raised

Figure 7: Rogier van der Weyden, Flemish, about 1400–1464, *Saint Luke Drawing the Virgin*, about 1435–40, oil and tempera on panel, 137.5 × 110.8 cm (54^1/$_8$ × 43^5/$_8$ in.).
Museum of Fine Arts, Boston, gift of Mr and Mrs Henry Lee Higginson, 93.153.
Photograph © 2008, Museum of Fine Arts, Boston.

parapet, their backs to the viewer. From this description it is clear that no simple linear timescale is in operation. The architecture, furnishings and the robes of the figures are all contemporary with van der Weyden's lifetime, yet the principal subjects were living 1,400 years before. Then again, although there was a long-standing tradition that Luke had formed his account of the birth and infancy of Jesus directly from Mary (a tradition founded upon Luke 1.2), there is no suggestion that he himself was present at any of the events he describes. That he was a physician by training, and a companion of the apostle Paul, is attested by the New Testament (Colossians 4.14; 2 Timothy 4.11), and it is generally accepted that he was the author of the Gospel which bears his name, and the Acts of the Apostles, but the tradition that he was an artist, in particular a painter of images of the Virgin, is difficult to trace back before the sixth century CE. Nonetheless it was a widely known and accepted tradition in the Middle Ages and probably not seriously questioned. Certainly there were artists' guilds under the patronage of the evangelist, and artists themselves were proud of the association of their skill with him.

So how do we interpret van der Weyden's painting? It is only possible to make sense of it through the concept of simultaneity which we outlined earlier. The action of the painting, and our part in it, transcends time and space. It is both in time and timeless. Luke is the artist–evangelist, a painter in words and of pictures. He gives honour to the Virgin and Child by his depiction of them in word and portrait. He is also every artist who uses his God-given gift in this way. He is thus, in a sense, van der Weyden – and in this particular painting it is recognized that Luke is a self-portrait – just as he is Gislebertus present in the Garden of Eden at the Fall, and at the awakening of the three Magi by the angel.

Conclusion

Though the events depicted have their place in historical time, because they are part of salvation-history they have their place in every time. So for van der Weyden or the anonymous artists of the Gloucester mural and the Sherborne triptych, to depict their characters in contemporary dress is quite correct; they are the men and women of every age, participants in what Hans Frei called the 'narrative web'. So Sir John Dwnn of Cydweli, his wife and daughter, can be seen in the company of the Blessed Virgin, St Catherine, St Barbara, St John Baptist and St John the Evangelist. This is because all are together in the one reality of the world and time-absorbing text of the biblical narrative, just as all those who have stood or kneeled before van der Weyden's painting and the Dwnn altarpiece are also present. Sir John Dwnn *is* in the company of the Virgin, Christ-child and the saints, just as we are with him, or with St Luke as he sketches the Virgin *Galactotrophousa* (the Milk-Giver) for one of the icons traditionally attributed to him. Indeed, it is not out of place to see the works of art we have been discussing as icons. They are sacramentals through which we as observers and participants are drawn into the presence of that which is depicted. Time and space are no barriers here.

We are participants whether we like it or not, or whether we realize it or not. Perhaps that is the message conveyed by the casually conversing couple in van der Weyden's painting, their backs turned to artist, subject and ourselves alike, seemingly oblivious of who or what is behind them. All who have lived, are living, and are yet to live, are in a reality which is *sub specie aeternitatis*, their lives bound up with that kingdom of heaven which, as the archaeologist Michael Costen observed, 'was to be found in every village'. When the faithful prayed in St Mary de Crypt in Gloucester, or the sick and aged lay before the Sherborne altarpiece, Sir John Dwnn and his household prayed before their domestic altar or the members of a guild of artists before van der Weyden's reredos, then they were there, present, at those events visually described. As St Gregory of Nyssa put it, history 'proceeds from beginnings to beginnings by successive beginnings that have no end'. There is no past in medieval art, only an eternal present.

Note

1. Edward Robinson, *Icons of the Present* (London, SCM Press, 1993), p. 2.

Suggested reading

B. S. Levy (ed.), *The Bible in the Middle Ages: Its Influence on Literature and Art* (New York: Binghampton, 1992).

Peter Lord, *The Visual Culture of Wales: Medieval Vision* (Cardiff: University of Wales Press, 2003).

Andreas Petzold, *Romanesque Art* (London: George Weidenfeld and Nicolson, 1995).

4

The Bible in the Italian Renaissance: Masaccio and Michelangelo as biblical exegetes

HEIDI HORNIK

Some of the best-known depictions of biblical paintings come from the period of the Renaissance. In this chapter, Heidi Hornik explores how the Bible is seen through the eyes of Masaccio and Michelangelo, two of the Renaissance's most important artists, and assesses their contribution to the visualizing of biblical narrative.

Introduction

The visual arts reflect and express the Bible in numerous ways that all begin with the mind and artistic talent of the artist who is interpreting the narratives. Artists throughout time have incorporated cultural, historical and contemporary religious issues into works that are based on biblical stories. The Italian Renaissance was a time of rediscovery of the antique worlds of Greece and Rome, an unsettled period of religious upheaval and significant scientific, architectural and political advancements. The fifteenth century saw the discovery of one-point linear perspective (the depiction in a realistic sense of a third dimension on a two-dimensional wall or panel), advanced techniques in the study of optics, and the completion of Brunelleschi's dome over the Florentine cathedral. The sixteenth century was the time of Pope

Julius II who commissioned the Sistine Chapel ceiling from Michelangelo and the painting of his private papal apartments by Raphael. The Reformation emerged, forcing a split on Western Christianity that evoked a response by the Roman Catholic Church in the Council of Trent (1545–63).

This chapter focuses on two artists, Masaccio and Michelangelo Buonarotti. Masaccio, a painter and artist, lived during the beginning of the Renaissance in fifteenth-century Florence. Michelangelo, a High Renaissance master, who excelled in sculpture, painting and architecture, worked mainly in Florence and Rome. Both of these artists were involved in major commissions for wealthy patrons who wanted elaborate fresco cycles done in their honour or that of their families. Masaccio's Brancacci Chapel in Santa Maria del Carmine depicts scenes from the life of Peter (the namesake of the patron Piero Brancacci) taken from Acts and the Gospel of Matthew. Michelangelo's Sistine Chapel ceiling continues the complex iconographic programme of the pope's private chapel with scenes from Genesis. Particular examples from each of these famous and extensive fresco cycles are discussed. Michelangelo's *David* depicted a well-established tradition of a Florentine civic symbol. His depictions of *David* and *Moses* (commissioned for Pope Julius II, the patron of the Sistine Chapel ceiling) serve as sculptural examples of how the Bible was expressed in the visual arts.

Masaccio and early Renaissance painting[1]

The Trinity, Lenzi Chapel, Santa Maria Novella, Florence

The Florentine artist Masaccio (1401–28) is sometimes called the founder of Renaissance painting. Despite his short life of only 27 years, his art was innovative, creative and moved the entire city of Florence into a Renaissance. His paintings used one-point linear perspective and his figures were three-dimensional with individual personalities evident through their facial features, gesture and emotions. Masaccio painted

The Trinity in fresco in the Franciscan church of Santa Maria Novella, Florence, for the Lenzi family. In 1425, Masaccio was called upon to construct the fresco, a painting on wet plaster, using the most advanced techniques in painting. His friendships with two intellectual leaders of the Florentine community, Brunelleschi (1377–1446) and Leon Battista Alberti (1404–72), enabled him to incorporate scientific perspective into a painting for the first time in history. Filippo Brunelleschi, an architect, had devised a system of one-point linear perspective in the church of San Lorenzo, Florence. The lines (called orthogonals) of the nave and clerestory windows converged on the altar to visually guide the congregant's eye. Alberti, a humanist, writer and architect himself, later codified these theories in *Della Pittura* (1435 Latin; 1436 Italian) and dedicated this book to Masaccio. Masaccio had the benefit of the input of both of these architects on how perspective was done in three-dimensional space, but it was his application of these new principles of perspective to a two-dimensional surface that changed the course of painting. He also employed scientific linear perspective to *The Tribute Money* in the Brancacci Chapel, discussed below.

The composition is, literally and figuratively, 'framed' by a marble barrel vault with pink limestone cornice and capitals. The barrel vault with recessed coffers inside is a direct reference to the Roman building type used in the Pantheon (118–25 CE) and the Basilica of Constantine (310–20 CE). The orthogonals of the painting extend the lines of the coffered ceiling of the barrel vault and converge at the foot of the cross in the centre of the painting. The corners of the base of the painting also converge at the same point. This is eye level for a 5′10″ person standing 30 feet (10 metres) out into the nave of the church. The vanishing point or place of convergence is on the horizon line. Things going into the distance converge. This allows every object to be perspected relative to another. This method created a new way of producing painting that required that every artist had to be educated in mathematics. Masaccio created a grid pattern on the surface that broke from the traditional underdrawing on plaster. The grid system required the entire composition to be worked out geometrically.

The religious iconography was also highly innovative. There are four levels charged with biblical symbolism. The upper level or heavenly level shows the three Persons of the Trinity. God the Father is portrayed as an elderly man dressed in a red gown with blue mantle. The Holy Spirit takes the form of the dove and is placed between God and Christ. Christ is visible on the cross. As one's eye continues down the length of the cross, one moves to the second or saintly level. Mary, the mother of Christ, is seen on his favoured side or to the viewer's left. She is dressed in the traditional blue robes and gestures to the viewer to move their attention away from her and back to the Crucifixion. Opposite Mary is John the Beloved, taken from the Gospel of John. The Renaissance artists seemed to favour the Crucifixion story as told by John, as Mary and John the Beloved are the most popular figures to be painted at the foot of the cross (see John 19.26–27). The donor or fourth level creates a rectangle in the lower half of the painting. On the viewer's left are the patrons of the composition, Signor and Signora Lenzi. Signor Lenzi was a Florentine official in 1425 and he is depicted wearing the cap and garment of this position. They kneel outside the recessed chapel space that contains all the other figures discussed so far.

The majority of the composition displays the three Persons of the Trinity in a correctly perspected painted space showing the latest advances in painting of the day. Perhaps the most interesting area of the fresco is the lower or ground level that is often described as portraying the first anatomically correct skeleton. Signor and Signora Lenzi are placed directly above this painted sarcophagus. The Italian inscription written above the sarcophagus translates, 'What you are, I once was. What I am, you will become.' The skeleton is not only Everyman or Death personified, but becomes a representation of the first Adam. The tradition that Christ was crucified at the very place that Adam was buried was well known and frequently depicted in art.

The death of Christ, the Second Adam, expiated the sin of the first, and as such, the fresco was a visualization of St Paul's argument in Romans 5 where Christ as the Second Adam came to 'undo' what the first Adam had done, the one through whom sin had entered the world (Romans 5.12–19). The first Adam was himself also the first man to be saved by Christ's blood that seeps down from the upper portion of the fresco towards Adam. As the words of Adam, and not Death or Everyman, the epithet takes on another meaning. Adam says, 'What you are – human beings with a stubborn and wilful inclination to sin – I once was; what I am – a sinner redeemed by God's grace and the sacrificial death of his Son – you will become.' The Christian gospel proclaims that Death does not have the final word in this life (1 Corinthians 15).

In great art, as in great literature, the spectator seeks his or her place in the story to understand its relevance, and in art, as in literature, may at various times assume multiple roles. In Masaccio's fresco, the viewer may adopt the patron's posture of reverence in the presence of the Triune God, and surely experience the pathos of St John's mourning over the suffering of Christ crucified. The individual recognition that the Lenzi will, in fact, become skeletons stresses their own mortality. This artistic patronage by the Lenzi is also intended as assistance in their ultimate salvation after their death. The iconography of the dead continues today in the statement and prayer, 'Pray for the dead and the dead will pray for you.' The acknowledgement of their eventual death reiterates their hope of ultimate salvation through their commitment in the decoration of the Dominican church of Santa Maria Novella.

The spectator may also relate to Mary, the ideal witness, who points to Christ crucified. Mary looks directly at the viewer and gestures us to contemplate the scene. And surely this Mary, as ideal witness to her Son's suffering on behalf of humanity, is a role that the audience relates to today just as they did 500 years ago. God the Father lovingly supports his Son in his suffering and at the same time fixes the viewer/worshipper with a gaze no less penetrating than the mother's. Whereas many detractors of Christianity would point to the Crucifixion as evidence of the absurdity of the Trinity, Masaccio, and many Trecento artists before him, claim it is in this very same moment that the essential unity of Father, Son and Holy Spirit is most clearly revealed. Here there is no depiction of God turning his back on his Son, disgusted at the sight of one who at that moment bore all the sins of the world. Instead, the viewer sees a loving Father, who in the mystery of the Trinity is at one with the Son and the Spirit, and suffers on our behalf.

Masaccio has thus creatively combined contemporary events (the newly discovered scientific linear perspective), biblical narrative (Crucifixion), theological doctrine (the Trinity) and patronage (Lenzi dressed as a fifteenth-century Florentine official) into one of the most celebrated church frescoes for over 500 years.

The Tribute Money, Brancacci Chapel, Santa Maria del Carmine, Florence

Masaccio worked on the Brancacci Chapel late in his short life along-side Masolino (1383–1447), who may have been his teacher. Pietro Brancacci (d. 1366–7) founded the chapel and it was passed to his nephew Felice Brancacci, who was the legal owner during the time that Masaccio and Masolino painted a Peter cycle on its walls. Filippino Lippi finished the fresco cycle in the early 1480s. The chapel was restored in the 1980s, and after the grime was removed colours reminiscent of Giotto were revealed. Both artists respected the Trecento master and his ability to produce significant and beautiful fresco cycles in Padua and Assisi. Renaissance artists felt tradition and method were very important and admired the work of their predecessors. The next generation continued this sentiment when Michelangelo came to the Brancacci Chapel to study the manner in which Masaccio painted gesture, drapery and lifelike figures in motion.

This was a funerary chapel and its function was to present frescoes in such a way that, by glorifying God, one would be able to worry less about the salvation of one's soul. Once again, Masaccio uses classical architecture to arrange the space with a constant sense of the viewer's space and viewing point. The three-dimensional moulded cornice surrounding the chapel, for example, is completely flat and therefore a painted illusion. A window that generated natural light was integrated into the composition along with Masaccio's placement of shadow in the various paintings.

The iconographic programme of the chapel is a Peter cycle, perhaps in honour of the founding father's patron saint and/or related to the history of the Carmelite Order. It was very common for the clergy to play a part in the theological programme of a chapel. Masaccio and Masolino worked separately on the fresco scenes but attribution issues remain. Both artists painted major rectangular scenes on the side walls and smaller, vertical panels on the interior wall of the chapel. The other painted scenes include the most famous composition of *The Tribute Money* by Masaccio, where Peter appears three times in order to relate most effectively the various parts of the progressive narrative. Depicting a scene unique to Matthew's Gospel (Matthew 17.24–27), Peter stands by Christ's side as the tax collector arrives; he bends over and takes a coin from the mouth of a fish. In the third and final scene and that which was favoured by Michelangelo, Peter gives the coin to the tax collector. Peter is an artistic 'type' and can be easily identified in all of the compositions: he was depicted as an older, bearded man with heavy, layered robes and a majestic stance.

Peter Healing with his Shadow, Brancacci Chapel, Santa Maria del Carmine, Florence

Peter Healing with his Shadow (Plate 5) is a very rare subject in the history of art. Technically, prior to Masaccio's knowledge of light, depth and perspective, depicting shadows was not known and perhaps this is the reason why they were not painted. Now that cast shadows could be painted – and the fact that the programme was from the life of Peter – it seemed natural to include the healing miracle. The story is taken from the Acts of the Apostles (5.12–14) but it is set in a fifteenth-century Florentine alley. The rusticated walls of the back of a Renaissance palazzo can be recognized on the left side of the painting. Overhanging back rooms on struts are also visible. It is a vertical composition as it flanked the left side of the organ wall.

Peter walks past the two lame men on the side of the street but does not seem to notice them. Yet the power of his presence through his shadow heals them as it falls upon them. The healing scenes by the apostles in the Book of Acts parallel those by Christ in Luke's Gospel. This erect and almost regal body position and facial expression is a stark contrast to the kneeling man whose body has aged less gracefully; he has even lost his hair, while the younger man has lost the use of his legs entirely and lies across the dirty alleyway. Some art historians believe that this younger, almost prostrate man may be a self-portrait of the artist. We know little about the personal life of Masaccio but, if he placed himself in a position of illness or weakness, one may assume that he was modest in respect to the task he had of painting the acts of such an important figure as Peter, the first Bishop of Rome.

Healing at the time of Jesus and the apostles was an incredibly important concern for people. Due to the lack of a health care system in antiquity, illness was often a precursor to death. A weakened individual was sometimes shunned by the community for fear of infection or inability to contribute to the continued health of the group. Masaccio, the Carmelite Order and the Brancacci family gave us a visual narrative to reflect upon, not only in relation to the physical healing powers of Peter but also in relation to the need of spiritual healing on the part of the viewer – both then and now.

Michelangelo and the High Renaissance

Michelangelo Buonarotti (1475–1564) excelled in sculpture, painting and architecture and left over 500 letters and 300 poems as indications of his love of writing. He was born on 6 March 1475 in the Florentine outpost of Caprese in the Tiber valley. When he was one month old his family moved to Settignano, a small town just outside of Florence that was known for its large population of stonecutters. Both his uncle and father objected to him becoming an artist as it was beneath his social class, but he was apprenticed to Domenico Ghirlandaio at the age of 13 in 1488. Our information about Michelangelo comes from his own written material and two biographical sources, Giorgio Vasari (1550 and 1568) and Ascanio Condivi (1553). Both men held Michelangelo in the highest regard. Vasari states that Michelangelo learned to integrate his observation of nature, his fresco technique and the use of antique sources into his works from Ghirlandaio. It should also be added that the Ghirlandaio workshop probably also taught Michelangelo the biblical narratives so often depicted in Renaissance altarpieces and fresco cycles. Ghirlandaio was famous for producing religious works commended for their theological accuracy and artistic style.

Michelangelo lived in the Palazzo Medici and often ate at table with Lorenzo de'Medici during the years 1489–90. It was there that he learned from humanists such as Angelo Poliziano and leading clerics including Giovanni de'Medici, who would become Pope Leo X. Michelangelo also had access to the Medici sculpture garden that was kept in nearby San Marco. Lorenzo de'Medici was an avid collector of Roman and Greek antiquities. Michelangelo left Florence in 1494 when the Medici were exiled. He travelled north, returned briefly to

Florence in 1495, and then was in Rome from 1496 to 1501. At this time he sculpted the Vatican *Pietà* for the tomb of the French cardinal Jean de Bilheres Lagraulas. Michelangelo accepted the commission for the *David* (discussed on p. 75) in 1501 in Florence. The *David* was completed in 1504.

The Sistine Chapel Ceiling, Sistine Chapel, Rome

Michelangelo, who preferred to sculpt rather than to paint, could not turn this commission down. Pope Julius II della Rovere (1503–13) 'requested' that Michelangelo continue the decoration of his private chapel. Giuliano, who took the name Julius II with an apparent reference to Julius Caesar, was a very generous patron of the arts. This extensive patronage was normal and expected at this time. Julius II was elected pope because of his statements regarding reform of a troubled Church: the hedonistic lifestyle of Pope Alexander VI, in particular, was out of the question. Julius II required a new visual language to represent the accomplishments and tradition of the Roman Catholic Church. The extension of the Church into the Americas and Southern and Eastern Asia was part of the motivation of this self-aggrandized pope (who used Roman imperial models for his artistic commissions) in his desire to leave the world some of the most famous works of art.

The Sistine Chapel was built in the 1480s by Julius's uncle, Pope Sixtus IV. It was built within the Vatican palace and was meant to accommodate the increasing size of the papal court and in order to have a location to house the conclaves of cardinals that met to select a pope. It was, and still remains, the pope's private chapel that can be closed (much to modern tourists' dismay) whenever he decides that he needs to use it. Sixtus commissioned artists from Florence and Umbria to paint the chapel walls with scenes from the lives of lawgivers Jesus and Moses. The overall programme of the chapel is as follows: scenes from 'The World before the Law' are found in the Genesis ceiling scenes of 1508–12; 'The World during the Law' is depicted on the

1480s side walls and depicts Old Testament scenes from the life of Moses. The New Testament narratives from the life of Jesus constitute 'The World after the Law' and were completed when Michelangelo returned (1534–41) to paint the *Last Judgement* above the altar on the west chapel wall.

Michelangelo's painted ceiling (Plate 6) is composed of nine bays that are divided into three triads: *The Creation of the World* (Genesis 1), *The Creation of Man* (Genesis 1–3) and *The Noah stories* (Genesis 6–9). Michelangelo painted the scenes from the east entrance towards the altar. He began with the Noah triad: *The Drunkenness of Noah* (Genesis 9.20–27), *The Flood* (Genesis 7.17–24; 8.6–8) and *The Sacrifice of Noah* (Genesis 8.20–22). These scenes are multifigured and more difficult to see from the ground than the other six scenes. Vasari told a tale of how Michelangelo painted these three scenes on the scaffolding and when he had finished came down, saw that they were too small and enlarged all the figures. This is probably not the case but makes for an interesting story!

The next triad includes *The Original Sin and Expulsion from the Garden of Eden, The Creation of Eve* and *The Creation of Adam.* The left side of the temptation and expulsion scene (Genesis 3.1–24) shows the moment of temptation as the serpent, wrapped around the thick trunk of the tree of knowledge, passes the fruit to Eve. Sin is born in Michelangelo's rocky landscape of the Garden of Paradise. This is not the green, flowery image of Paradise that most of us have as we think of Paradise. Rather, Michelangelo filled the composition with boulders and leaves. The drama of the expulsion is heightened by the anguish visible in the faces of the sinful and the barren green land behind them.

The theological programme demands that attention be paid to the place of morality in the landscape of creation stories. God forms the world through light and dark. He separates the land and the waters and makes the birds and the fish. *The Creation of Adam* (Genesis 1.26–27; 2.7–8) is one of the most famous images in Western culture.

It is set with Adam reclining on a rock formation and God in a cloud surrounded by figures whose identity remains an enigma to scholars. The creation of woman is placed in the central scene of the ceiling in a chapel dedicated to Mary and for the Roman Church which sees Mary as the new Eve and mother of all things in nature and humanity. The Noah triad is also heavily dependent on a visual landscape to tell the story of the flood, the drunkenness of Noah, and the salvation of humanity.

The colour restored during the cleaning in the 1980s reveals an intense and innovative technique that is applied in broad areas and uses *changeant* or changing colours in one area. *The Cangiante* technique places different colours side by side to create highlighting effects on drapery that reminds one of the reflection of light on shot-silk. The iconography depicts a complex pattern of Old Testament exegesis but the ceiling is also a source of inspiration for generations of painters because of its innovative colour techniques.

The Creation of Eve (Genesis 1.27; 2.20–25) is the central scene of the ceiling and the pivotal scene in term of importance. To the right of the Creation of Eve scene is the Cumaean sybil. Virgil's *4th Eclogue* foretells that a saviour will be born under the age of peace that is often understood to be the reign of Augustus. As stated above, Julius II also believed that his age was a Golden Age.

The final triad painted is the first chronologically in the Bible. *The Separation of Light from Darkness* (Genesis 1.4) is closest to the altar and represents the first day of creation. *The Creation of Sun, Moon and Planets* (Genesis 1.10–11 and 14–16) depicts the acts of the third and fourth day. *The Separation of the Waters* (Genesis 1.6–8; 20–22) shows the activity that took place from the second to the fifth days. The panels alternated in size. Those smaller bays had painted pairs of *nudes* with medallions and oak-leaves (a reference to the family coat of arms of the della Rovere popes that may have been a pun). The pendentives, or triangular areas, were planned to have apostles but instead Michelangelo painted seven *prophets* and five *sibyls*. Christ's ancestors are located in the lunettes and spandrels.

Some art historians believe that Michelangelo was given free rein by Pope Julius II to develop and paint the iconography of the ceiling. Others think that Julius would have consulted his many theological advisors at least for the iconography. Julius did instruct Michelangelo to carry the ceiling decoration 'down to the histories on the lower part'; so whoever ultimately devised the programme, it contributed to the Sistine Chapel iconographic design of representing the history of the Church on earth.

Italian Renaissance sculpture

David

Michelangelo's *David* was the most colossal of sculptures in a long line of iconographically significant representations of the Old Testament figure. Donatello, the early Renaissance sculptor, executed a marble, 6′3″ work that was placed in front of a wall painted blue and decorated with gold fleurs-de-lys in the Palazzo della Signoria, Florence, in 1416. The Palazzo was the main governmental palace of the city and the other decorations behind it were also symbols of Florence. David remains a metaphor for the city. He was fierce in his ability to protect the freedoms of his people from strong external forces. Florence used this symbolism as the city was constantly under siege from more formidable foes – the papal armies of Rome, the Sienese and the Pisans.

In the 1460s, Piero de'Medici commissioned another *David* by Donatello and housed it in the private context of the Palazzo Medici. This now appropriated the civic imagery to the powerful Medici family. The *David* was first recorded in 1469 in a description of the wedding celebrations of Piero's son Lorenzo to Clarice Orsini. The *David*, placed on a columnar base in the palace courtyard, was visible from the street. The Medici wanted a dynasty much like the respected ruler in the Old Testament who became King David. This sculpture and Old Testament figure provided a city, and a family with powerful imagery of rulership and dynasty. This 1460s sculpture was the first life-size, freestanding, bronze male nude since antiquity and is described as a classical ephebe or pre-pubescent boy. Donatello combined the biblical text with the classical forms of heroism and created a symbol for the Medici and for Florence.

In 1501, again in Florence, Michelangelo was commissioned by the Opera del Duomo and the consul of the Wool Guild to reclaim the civic imagery that had been taken by a private family. His *David* was originally commissioned for the north part of the cathedral. The block of marble was badly damaged and had lain in the cathedral workshop since 1466. Michelangelo completed the 17'⅛" marble sculpture in 1504 and it was placed to the left of the entrance to the main governmental palace, the Palazzo della Signoria. So, once again, Florence had recovered the coveted figure of David. Still today, the 'Davide falso', the famous copy, stands in that original position. Michelangelo's *David* was cleaned in 2004 on the 500th anniversary of its completion. It had remained outside for 360 years and this prolonged exposure to the weather, combined with a cleaning in 1843 with hydrochloric acid, caused it to lose much of its original lustre and polish. It may also have looked quite different in the sixteenth century. One art historian recounts that in October 1504 the tree stump supporting the David was gilded in gold, a gilt garland was placed on the figure's head and a belt of 28 gilt bronze leaves was around his waist.

The colossal, three times life-size figure combined the beauty and proportion of antique sculptures from the Golden Ages of Rome and Greece with the greatness of Florence. The nudity is often questioned. 1 Samuel 17.38–39 certainly does not interpret David as being nude before his fight with Goliath. So one may ask what Michelangelo was thinking of in this meditative, pre-fight colossus: the pose of the figure, the maturity of the body and the nudity suggest the classical hero Hercules. Placing a Hercules-like David at the entrance to the Palazzo della Signoria or in the cathedral of the city (its intended location) created a powerful civic connotation. Hercules had appeared on the state seal of Florence since the end of the thirteenth century, so also had a history as a symbol of Florence. Michelangelo did not give any attributes to his *David*, allowing the viewer to incorporate a wide range of civic and religious references.

Moses

In Italian Renaissance art, Moses is usually depicted as an older, bearded man. This distinguished 'type' of image for the lawgiver who communicated directly with God on Mount Sinai on several occasions also has horns. The horns have an interesting history. According to Exodus 34.29, when Moses came down from Mount Sinai rays of light emanated from his head. The Hebrew word *qeren* (meaning both horns and rays) signifies power. St Jerome translated *qeren* into *cornuta* which is the Latin Vulgate translation for horns. There are many theories as to why St Jerome did this but most scholars of the Hebrew Bible think that Jerome wanted to continue the intention of the original writer of Exodus 34.29. This deliberate mistranslation, however, became deeply imbedded in the iconography of Christian art.

By the sixteenth century, the time of Michelangelo's work illustrated here (Figure 8), the visual tradition was firmly in place. The tourist who views Michelangelo's sculpture in the church of San Pietro in Vincoli, Rome, may be told that Moses has just descended from the mountain or that he is angry at the Israelites for worshipping the golden calf. Instead, can we look at Moses in the proper context of the sculpture? Michelangelo's original commission from Pope Julius II della Rovere was to sculpt 30 over-life-size figures for the Pope's three-storey free-standing tomb (23′6″ × 35′6″) in St Peter's Basilica. This monument was to be over an internal oval burial chamber. It was patterned after Roman imperial funeral pyres and would have had a figure of the deceased at the top. The lowest level had niches and sculptures on all sides. Each niche was to be flanked by an over-life-size marble nude. Six of the projected 16 nudes were begun. Each corner of the middle level had a seated figure. They were to depict Moses and St Paul, and the personification of the active and contemplative life.

The tomb was scaled down and relocated after Julius' death and Michelangelo brought only three sculptures to a near-completed state. *Moses*, one of those three, was originally intended to be on the second of a three-storey design in a corner position. *Moses* was to incorporate the same ideals of leadership – priest, lawgiver and ruler – that Pope Sixtus IV had specified for the 1480s wall frescoes in the Sistine Chapel. The intention was to view him from below. Today, he sits in a ground-level position on the revised monument completed in 1545. Like Michelangelo's *David*, intended to be in the north of the Florence cathedral, the torso of *Moses* is proportionally too long when viewed on eye level. *Moses* was carved for optical correctness that is completely lost today. His upper torso was to be more dramatic as it rose from his waist. The drapery, intended to be flowing and elaborate, now seems bulky and overdone.

The monumentality given to Moses in his current position prompts the overzealous, but misinformed, tour guide to talk about the Moses in the Exodus 34.29 context instead of the holder of the Tablets of the Law who looks outward towards his people with prophetic inspiration. Moses has learned from his experience with God, but there is much ahead. Perhaps that is why it is also so common that Moses be aged with long beard and hair. As a symbol of the wilderness generation, Michelangelo's *Moses* retains the strength and fortitude necessary for these post-Mount Sinai activities. Prophetic wisdom, for the viewer, comes with age.

Pope Julius II intended to be buried in St Peter's to connect himself permanently with the first pope, Peter, who was buried there. This association with the past would further underscore the apostolic

Figure 8: Michelangelo, *Moses* (1515).
San Pietro in Vincoli, Rome.

succession of the popes from Peter (Matthew 16.18–19). The Julius II tomb is located in San Pietro in Vincoli, Rome.

Conclusion

The Italian Renaissance was a time of scientific discovery and human innovation. It was a time when humanists and scientists worked hand-in-hand to understand the world in which they lived while still maintaining their religious convictions. Philosophers, painters, musicians, sculptors, writers, architects looked to the cultures of Ancient Greece and Rome for ideas, information and theories. It was a rebirth of thought and technique that fed into a society eager to create and innovate. Masaccio and Michelangelo were trained in the workshop tradition in Florence that including drawing from nature, the basic technique of colour and the manipulation of light and shadow. They learned how to use the media of charcoal, tempera and fresco. Michelangelo also used oil for his paintings. In addition to these artistic skills, they also were active members of Florentine parishes, attended Mass daily and studied the established visual tradition of biblical narratives. Only after a high level of skill in the artistic techniques and knowledge of the biblical narratives could they become the innovative geniuses in religious paintings that are recognized today.

The great minds of the Italian Renaissance culture included at the top of the list artists who were steeped in the religious tradition of Roman Catholicism. Their works required extensive knowledge not only of the biblical narratives but also of the liturgical practices of the Mass. Only after this education could they create some of the greatest masterpieces of Western tradition and Western religion in the history of humankind.

Note

1 All of the works discussed in this chapter that are not illustrated may be viewed on the website <www.wga.hu/index1.html> (accessed 23 March 2007). Please search by artist followed by the title or location of the work discussed.

Suggested reading

Heidi J. Hornik and Mikeal C. Parsons, *Illuminating Luke: The Infancy Narrative of Christ in Italian Renaissance Painting*, Vol. 1 (Harrisburg, London, New York: Trinity Press International, 2003).

Heidi J. Hornik and Mikeal C. Parsons, *Illuminating Luke: The Public Ministry of Christ in Italian Renaissance Painting*, Vol. 2 (London and New York: T.&T. Clark International, 2005).

Robert B. Kruschwitz (ed.), *Christian Reflection: A Series in Faith and Ethics* (Waco, TX: Center for Christian Ethics, Baylor University, 2000–7).

5

Icons:
The silent gospels

ANDREAS ANDREOPOULOS

The depiction of biblical characters and scenes in the art of Eastern Christianity is handled in a much different way than in the West. In this chapter, Andreas Andreopoulos outlines the historical and theological perspectives required by the viewer in order to appreciate fully the distinctive way biblical narrative has been visualized in the Orthodox tradition.

Introduction

Liturgical practices in the Christian East have always been associated with a kind of sensory richness that many Westerners find difficult to understand. Many Western Christians find a plain church environment conducive to prayer and reflection on the biblical message, but when they enter a candle-lit, fragrant Byzantine church, the walls of which are completely covered with icons, they often find the sensory over-load distracting from what is more familiar to them, namely a religious environment that is centred essentially on the written and spoken word. But Eastern Christianity developed a different language of liturgical worship, in which icons, smells, candles and music are merely elements that direct the attention of the faithful towards the biblical message and its elaboration, and not away from it. A Greek

who enters a Byzantine church in order to pray, or in order to participate in the liturgy, is very aware that he or she steps into an environment where everything, from the architecture of the building to the
regularity of the censing, carries a specific theological 'direction' that
is not distracting or simply decorative but, on the contrary, makes it
possible for him or her to worship God fully and with a correct
attitude. Through an appreciation of visual worship, we can discover
how iconography encourages the faithful to consider the biblical
message as it is understood within the tradition of the wider Church
and how to integrate it into their liturgical life.

It is perhaps unfortunate that icons in our time are usually only
associated in the West with the religious tradition of Orthodox countries such as Greece, Russia, Romania and Bulgaria. Admittedly, in the
last seven centuries or so, the West has developed a different language
of visual religious expression, but the art of iconography was part of
the spiritual tradition of the entire Church, Eastern and Western, for
many centuries, and as such it belongs to all Christendom. It is true,
too, that almost at the same time as iconography was becoming
important in the East in determining the orthodoxy of emperors and
patriarchs, the West was starting to explore different forms of artistic
and spiritual expression.

Much of the period of the Middle Ages does not hold an equally
important position in the hearts and the minds of Westerners as it does
for Easterners. While a Western historian may reminisce about the
'Dark' Ages, a Greek will think of the glory of Byzantium, one of the
most inspiring chapters in Eastern history. Naturally, then, anything
that comes from such an era will make a completely different impact
on the Western and Eastern mind. Nevertheless, the cultural contrast
between the Greek East and the Latin West is somewhat blurred in our
day, as historians and theologians look to both sides of the divide for
the sources of our culture and Christian heritage. Since the Christian
faith is something that stands above ethnic and cultural differences,
icons are part of the common medieval tradition and as such they may

be claimed by all Christians throughout the world. Orthodox Christianity may have preserved the symbolism of icons and the veneration of God and the saints through them, but in doing so it acted on behalf of all Christendom. Therefore, due to the current climate of ecumenical dialogue which frequently avoids a confrontational approach and tries instead to make the tradition of each side known to the other, icons are nowadays admired and appropriated more and more by Western Christians. They should feel entitled to use them, as one is entitled to appropriate a forgotten, but not lost, family legacy.

Icons are not simply religious decorations or even religious paintings. The abstract and emaciated look of the faces of the saints and their intense eyes that stare directly into the mind and the heart of the viewer, the flat surfaces, the lack of shadows and the golden background are not merely stylistic characteristics that give a 'spiritual look' to icons and identify them as objects that may be used in a church setting, but are visual approximations of the kingdom of heaven. Even small details can show this: the small and closed mouths of the saints – because no sound or verbal communication is needed in the kingdom of God; the big ears – suggesting that they hear our prayers; the absence of any shadows – because all is bathed in light in the kingdom of God; the illumination that comes from the inside and not from any external source – because the spiritual light of God is not the same as the physical light of the sun.

This helps us situate the icon within its proper framework; in other words, in reflecting on the historicity of the icon, we should always keep in mind that it is not a historical artefact intended to reflect the world of its time, nor does it try to reflect consciously something from the past. An icon does not try to reproduce a historical event as it could have been experienced by an eyewitness but, rather, it seeks to show that event first as it may appear from the perspective of God and second in a way that includes the experience of the living Church.

Icons and historical realism

This might suggest that a visually faithful representation of a biblical event is not necessarily consistent with the aims of iconography. If it had been possible for an eyewitness of the Crucifixion of Jesus to take a snapshot of the scene on Calvary, we would have a visual relic that would be invaluable for historical and archaeological reasons, but it would be completely useless from the point of view of iconography. This photograph would depict a dying man on a cross, or three dying men on three crosses, and possibly also a multitude of people crying from a distance, unable to come closer to their tortured relatives and, most likely, not daring to defy the menacing Roman soldiers. The scene would be identical to many other executions of criminals at any time or place. It would be extremely difficult, even for a trained archaeologist or theologian, to determine whether the man on the cross is Jesus, Spartacus or someone else. By itself it would reveal to us no more than a photograph of a modern execution by lethal injection or by firing squad would reveal.

An icon of the Crucifixion of Jesus, on the other hand, gives us a very different kind of information. To begin with, as is the case with every icon, the body of Christ is illuminated from the inside. Christ, even in death, retains his cruciform halo. The two thieves flanking him are not depicted in the same way: usually they are shown bound (instead of nailed) on their crosses, and their bodies are unnaturally contorted – especially the body of the unrepentant thief on the left. The icon brings together several episodes and characters into one scene that, according to the Gospel, did not take place at the same time: for example, the presence of Mary and John the Evangelist at the cross; the piercing of the side of Jesus; the three soldiers at the base of the cross who play dice; a soldier who breaks the legs of one of the thieves; the skull of Adam in a small opening under the cross; and a few people in burial clothes at the side, emerging from their graves. But often, too, the icon is rendered in a much simpler way, consisting only of the three central characters: the crucified Christ, Mary and John (Figure 9). Even the simplest types of the Crucifixion icon, however, include some strikingly non-realist elements, such as a depiction of angels at a distance, and a depiction of the sun and the moon (implying that even nature was shocked by the death of Christ on the cross). The simultaneous depiction of the trial, the Crucifixion and the Resurrection of Christ makes it possible for us to read the icon as a narrative. This is the first level of meaning in an icon, which simply consists of a visual representation of the biblical narrative, so that anyone who is familiar with the story can evoke its essential elements, based on the icon. Because of this, icons were sometimes thought of as a silent gospel, or the gospel of the illiterate. Even at this level, however, it must be noted that the naturalistic representation of the characters and the scene is secondary to the visual rendition of the Gospel narrative. Icons, therefore, frequently offer a condensed 'cinematic' view which does not correspond to only a frame from the supposed filming of the event, but to the entire film itself. From this perspective, the aim of the icon is to offer a visual version of the entire text, and not merely to represent a scene from the event as it could have been seen by an eyewitness – something that is by no means unknown to Western art.

As we examine an icon even further, we may discern several elements that are quite inconsistent with the textual sources. In the case of the icon of the Crucifixion, we may find such an element in the inscription above the cross. Although the four Gospels offer slightly different accounts of what was written in that inscription, all of them agree that it contained the phrase 'The King of the Jews' (Mark 15.26). Matthew adds the words 'This is Jesus' in front of it (Matthew 27.37), Luke adds 'This is' (Luke 23.38), and John adds 'Jesus of Nazareth' (John 19.19). The Johannine version is the source of the usual inscription in Western religious painting (INRI). The traditional Byzantine inscription, however, does not read the equivalent in Greek (*INBI*) as one would expect, but a completely different title with no scriptural basis: 'The King of Glory'.

Figure 9: *The Crucifixion* (eighteenth century). Russian icon.

This is an obvious example where iconography differs from the written text. The replacement of the Gospel inscription with the iconographic one is justified for several reasons. The most often-cited reason is that the inscription placed by the Romans on the cross served two purposes: to explain the reason for the execution of Jesus, and to mock and humiliate him. It does not, therefore, suggest the deeper reasons for the sacrifice of Christ on the cross, and it does not reflect its true dimensions in an appropriately majestic manner.

This does not explain fully, however, the change of the inscription and the choice of the new one. The sacrifice of Christ transformed the entire significance of the Crucifixion, one of the most shameful methods of execution in the Roman world, into a symbol of hope, glory and love. The inscription 'The King of the Jews', after all, is correct in a sense, unknown to the Romans who meant it as a mockery. Before we identify this as an example of a discrepancy between the written and the visual tradition, let us try to see what exactly the title 'King of Glory' means and where it comes from.

The word 'glory' is often used in John's Gospel, as a direct reference to the Crucifixion. This may be seen in 7.39 ('the Holy Spirit was not yet given, because Jesus was not yet glorified'), 12.16 ('his disciples did not understand these things at first; but when Jesus was glorified, then they remembered that these things were written about him and that they had done these things to him'), 12.23 ('the hour has come that the Son of Man should be glorified'), 17.1 ('Jesus spoke these words, lifted up his eyes to heaven, and said: "Father, the hour has come. Glorify your son, that your son also may glorify you"') and 21.19 ('this he spoke, signifying by what death he would glorify God'). The glorification of Christ through his Crucifixion, or the glorification of the Father through the Son in his Crucifixion, is an interpretation of the sacrifice of Christ on the cross, offered by the Gospel itself. The Crucifixion seen as an act of glorification, reflected in the title 'King of Glory', corresponds more accurately to the spirit of the Gospel than the title INRI. In other words, if we isolate the title

INRI in order to describe the Crucifixion, without making use of the biblical language that anticipated, prepared and interpreted the narrative of the Crucifixion, we commit the error of reading parts of the Gospel separately, and not in the context of the entire Gospel narrative. Iconography certainly does not make that mistake.

This example illustrates how the didactic narrative of the icon would not benefit from a historically correct re-creation of a biblical event; what the icon seeks to do is to express the *wider* narrative and theological interpretation of the Crucifixion.

Tradition and interpretation

This discrepancy between the historical view and the theological interpretation suggests a further question. How accurately does iconography attempt to portray the events described in the Gospel, in the light of the development of Christian theology? How much is iconography affected by theological developments? In other words, if we were to think of the Bible and the tradition of the Church as two different authoritative poles, which one is iconography closer to?

Having posed this question, I would now like to show why such a question would not make sense from the point of view of the iconographers. The early Church did not differentiate between the Bible and tradition. Until the time of Irenaeus of Lyons and Tertullian – the mid second century – there was no such thing as a canon that specified what the Christian Bible was. The issue of the canon was not finalized until the early fifth century. In fact, the terminology used at the institution of the canon suggests that what it tried to preserve was not the exact 'sayings' or the 'works' of Jesus, but the tradition of the Church as handed down by the apostles – the 'apostolic tradition'. This approach did not change significantly in the early Church or in Byzantium, and it was only much later that the tension between Scripture and tradition emerged as an issue. The tradition in which iconography was practised, to be sure, never saw any distinction between the two.

This means that, in practice, iconography is an expression of the Gospel as seen through the lens of the Holy Tradition: this was the only way in which the Gospel was understood at the time. Like the commentaries of the early church Fathers and the liturgical tradition, iconography was a depository of theological knowledge, the source and expression of theological thought. Icons always tried to give the complete view, rather than a partial depiction that could correspond literally to the biblical text, at the expense of its theological meaning. From the perspective of the iconographer (and any supervising priests), the theological views of the time were not considered to be additions to the biblical message, not separating intermediates, but as a way to bring us closer to it.

Icons, therefore, may be considered as a visual version of the living Gospel, the expression of which follows the development of the thought of the Church. This is the most significant factor in the evolution of iconographic types expressing biblical themes. Sometimes this evolution may involve relatively minor changes, such as the shape of a mandorla around the body of Christ, or the positions of the depicted persons relative to each other, but at other times it may result in completely different iconographic syntheses. The Resurrection of Christ, for instance, was represented by three different iconographic syntheses: the scene of the myrrh-bearing women meeting the angel at the empty tomb, based on Matthew 28, Mark 16, Luke 24 and John 20; the scene of Christ emerging from the tomb, which although the most popular paschal image in the West, has no biblical counterpart; and the scene of Christ descending to Hades, which although the main paschal image in the East, is based on an apocryphal narrative of the fourth century (the *Gospel of Nicodemus*).

It is interesting that both the Eastern and the Western tradition chose, as their main festal icons for Easter, images that do not correspond directly to the Gospel narratives. The absence of a specific Resurrection narrative in the Gospels, that is, a description of the

Resurrection itself, may be debated among biblical scholars, but in no way is the belief in the Resurrection of Jesus compromised within the Bible by this absence. The Resurrection is one of the central messages of the entire Bible, and yet its description or representation was not possible for many centuries. It was only after the Resurrection had securely entered spoken and written discourse that the taboo was relaxed and it could be represented visually. The East, however, despite the more prominent place it gave to the Resurrection of Christ in its theology, did not ever completely accept an explicit representation of the Resurrection. Although the iconographic synthesis of *The Emergence from the Tomb* was known in Byzantium since at least the ninth century, *The Descent into Hades*, the Byzantine festal icon of the Resurrection, is only indirectly connected with the Resurrection of Christ.

The icon of *The Descent into Hades* (Plate 7) shows Christ raising Adam and Eve from the tomb, and by extension, the entire humanity outside time, even the people who lived and died before the time of Christ. Death, or Hades, is depicted as a beaten and bound old man at the bottom, next to the broken gates of Hell. Sometimes this icon also includes a procession towards heaven. Since most of us are accustomed to the more usual image of *The Emergence from the Tomb*, we do not easily notice that *The Descent into Hades* does not represent the Resurrection of Christ directly. Instead, it represents the eternal Resurrection of the Church by Christ. This is consistent with the significance of the bodily Resurrection of Christ in the early Church, which was understood as the *continuous* Resurrection of Christ within the Church, and the *continuous* Resurrection of the Church as the body of Christ. The emphasis on the historical approach and the striving for historical accuracy that permeate modern theology were not known at the beginning of Christianity. The choice of *The Descent into Hades* as the festal icon of the Resurrection of Christ is a way of alluding to and respecting the absence in the Bible of any explicit description of this most glorious event in the history and theology of Christianity.

Theology and iconography

Examples like these, however, merely scratch the surface of the complex relationship between theology and iconography. We are used to thinking of theology as a system of ideas and doctrines that connect, lock into and explain each other, much in the way that a sociological or philosophical theory does. The very expression 'systematic theology' shows this somewhat mechanical tendency, although it has to be said that systematic theology or doctrinal theology or dogmatic theology is nothing new. It can be found in the literature of the early church Fathers such as John of Damascus and his *Exact Exposition of the Orthodox Faith*, written in the eighth century. Nevertheless, theological thought and informed spirituality is only partially taught, properly speaking, in a linear, systematic, academic manner. This does not mean that traditional spirituality consists of a sum of unrelated studies from the Bible and Holy Tradition. It simply means that for the Byzantine and the medieval mind it was not enough to ponder intellectually the mysteries of the faith, they had also to integrate them into their liturgical experience.

Of course, all spiritual traditions found ways to express their doctrines through some form of religious practice, prayer or meditation, but very often the theory or theology and the practice comprise different modes of spiritual activity. The occasional tension between *lex credendi* (the law of believing) and *lex orandi* (the law of praying) reflects this difficulty. The two modes are often bridged by the kind of liturgical and ritual practice that is informed both by theology and the study of Scripture, and also by prayer and meditation. Iconography, likewise, as a liturgical art that is defined by the *lex credendi* as much by the *lex orandi*, offers an interesting approach in this problem.

Let us think of a person who enters a church full of icons, in order to pray. Probably the first image one notices in a typical domed Byzantine church is the huge icon of Christ in Majesty (Pantokrator) on the dome (for an example, see Plate 8). The second most prominent place is in the apse, usually dedicated to the Mother of God in a pose of intercession. There are certain places where one can expect to find the icon of the patron saint of the church, or icons of the saints who wrote liturgical texts. In addition, there are two places where one can expect to see a series of icons directly inspired by the Gospel. In both situations, the icons do not express the Gospel stories literally, but rather according to the liturgical, festal time of the Church.

An almost linear exposition of the twelve major feasts of the year can be usually seen in the upper tier of the iconostasis. A careful observation of the order of the icons will show that in most cases they are not arranged according to a linear narrative principle that corresponds with the historical life of Christ, but according to the position of the feast they represent within the liturgical year. The Transfiguration, for instance, is placed after the Ascension of Christ, and not before the Crucifixion. The twelve-feast icon series is akin to a visual liturgical calendar.

The major depictions of the Gospel events, however, may be usually found in the upper levels of the church, below the dome. This level is also very often arranged in a liturgical fashion, but depending on the architecture of the particular church, those icons that depict the life of Christ, and other events described in the Gospels, are placed according to their theological significance. The placement of icons in a way that results in a theological reading is known as the iconographic 'programme' of a church. For instance, if there is enough space between the dome and the apse, the Epiphany may be placed on the north wall opposite the Transfiguration on the south, with the Nativity of Christ on the western wall and the Resurrection on the eastern, above the apse. This simple arrangement is an example that expresses the gradual manifestation of the divinity of Christ as light to the world. There are many different arrangements of icons in churches, corresponding to distinctive or specific theological or historical themes.

The placing of the image of the Mother of God holding the baby Jesus in a position relative to the icon of her Dormition, where Christ holds her soul in his arms as if it were a newborn baby, accentuates the Fatherhood of God. Usually, the icons flanking the entrance to the altar are, on the left side, an icon of the Mother of God holding the baby Jesus, and, on the right, an icon of Christ in Majesty, holding an open book. These images outline the entire trajectory of Christological salvation, from his Incarnation (suggested in his representation as a baby) until his Second Coming (suggested in his glorious appearance and in the open book). The space between these two icons, the doors of the altar, is where the priest (as the image of Christ) addresses the congregation. The doors of the altar are, appropriately, decorated with an icon of the Annunciation, the giving of the Word to the people.

All these liturgical connections demonstrate that in an iconographed church the Gospel is not merely represented in a visual form in the manner of the illuminations of a manuscript that accompany a biblical text. What we see is that the iconographic programme of a church creates a dynamic space where the images relate to one another offering a reading of the Gospel in liturgical space, in a way that no text would be able to achieve. The exposition of certain theological themes in three dimensions is augmented by the relative importance of the two main axes of the Byzantine church building: the top to bottom axis, which represents the hierarchy and the connection between heaven and earth, and the west to east axis, which represents the liturgical progression towards the end of time. The gaze of the spectator may move from icon to icon within this complex space, thus being able to take in almost simultaneously the entire reading of the Gospel and the economy of salvation in a powerful synthetic view. It is hard to see or even to imagine anything comparable in the visual arts, at least until the invention of virtual reality.

The Bible as an icon

There is an additional dimension to the relationship between iconography and the Bible. We generally think of iconography as a means of translating the Gospel into the language of images. Nevertheless, the use of icons in the Church is more accurately described by their role as mediums of veneration rather than as tools of instruction. This was one of the central issues in the iconoclastic debate, right from the beginning: aside from questions that dealt with which aspect of the hypostatic union of Christ, his simultaneous divinity and humanity, could be portrayed, the defenders of the icons pointed out that the honour one renders to an image goes to the prototype, and thus a person who venerates an icon venerates the one who is represented in it. This premise of venerating and addressing God, his angels and the saints through symbols is a cornerstone for the development of liturgical life. The Fathers saw the 'icon' as a theologically charged concept, in that the relationship between the prototype and its image reflected the relationship between the Father and the Son, or God and man. Relations 'according to iconic resemblance' were often used to describe the function of symbols in the Church. Even the written word was seen as an icon (or symbol) of that which it denoted – and this explains the reverence with which the Orthodox Church treats the Gospel as a physical object.

A visitor to an Orthodox service will be struck by the position of the Gospel in the liturgical life of the Church, not only as a collection of ancient documents that make the life and the work of Christ known to us, but also as an object of adoration. The Word of God does not only have a place of teaching in the Church, but it is venerated itself. The Gospel book is not just a source of information, but it is itself an object of veneration. In the services of the Orthodox Church it is featured prominently many times in this role: it is offered ritually to the faithful to venerate in Matins; it is placed prominently on the altar and elevated at the beginning of the Divine Liturgy; it is brought forth ceremoniously as it enters the altar during the Little Entrance of the Divine Liturgy, also known as the Entrance of the Gospel. The Gospel book is understood, in other words, as an *icon* of the word of God, and is treated in exactly this way in the church. We can see from this that an extended definition of iconography may include the use of material objects in general, in liturgical worship. This suggests that traditional iconography is best understood in its liturgical framework, and not just as a form of art.

Icons in the age of iPods

It should not be too difficult for the average Westerner to accept and appreciate iconography as a most important medieval form of art. Iconography, with its distinctive understanding of the biblical message embedded in it, should not be thought of as alien to Western culture. As much as an icon may evoke initially thoughts of 'Byzantium' and 'Orthodoxy', there is enough cultural memory in the West since the Middle Ages to stretch beyond these confines. In addition, although it is more usual to connect traditional iconography to icons made in the Byzantine or even in the ante-Giotto Italian style, illuminations such as those of the Lindisfarne Gospels, and frescoes such as the image of St Cuthbert on the walls of Durham Cathedral, are not essentially any different from the mosaic of the Transfiguration in Sinai, or the Constantinopolitan icon of the Mother of God, known as Mary of Vladimir.

But even if we agree that iconography has as much right to exist in the West as it does in the East, how can it possibly speak to the present age? Is there anything in our age that makes icons more relevant to the West, considering that the West managed to develop quite a sophisticated and spiritual theology perfectly well without the assistance of icons? In addition, and in order to return to the central theme of this chapter, how can iconography possibly contribute to our understanding and dissemination of the biblical message?

Iconography as a practice and religious tradition was lost to the West for centuries. One of the most unexpected results of the Russian communist revolution, however, was that many Russian intellectuals and theologians who migrated to Western Europe after 1917 brought with them the visual tradition of icons, and they re-introduced it to the West. Although Greek and Russian immigrant communities had existed in the West for a long time, this wave of immigrants – who left their country of origin in order to preserve their intellectual and spiritual hypostasis, and not for the usual economic reasons – got involved quickly with the Western European (mostly French, but also English) society of artists, theologians and intellectuals. Theologians such as Mikhail Bulgakov and Georges Florovsky, and artists such as Wassily Kandinsky and Igor Stravinsky, 'conditioned' the West in matters Orthodox. At the same time, Greek artists such as Photis Kontoglou and Yannis Tsarouchis started rediscovering the legacy of iconography; in addition, people such as Stratis Teriade, a Greek based in France, supported some of the greatest Western artists in the first half of the twentieth century and discovered traditional Greek painting. Teriade established lasting links between the Greek tradition and Western Europe. Iconography was gradually introduced to the West, perhaps for the first time at the level of serious artistic discourse.

Icons entered once more in this way into the artistic collective memory of the West, but it is perhaps in the context of postmodernism that they can reclaim their spiritual content even outside the Church. With the celebrated 'collapse of the big narratives', we are much more ready now than ever to look at expressions of visual culture as equally valid expressions of thought, and as depositories of knowledge. Strangely, icons fit very well within the framework of postmodernist art, for many reasons:

- As they are constructed according to the principles of spiritual senses (the theological view of understanding biblical events), they are a commentary both on seeing and on the semiotics of seeing.

Similarly, the contemporary opening of the work of art so that it reveals and comments on the process that created it is an essential characteristic of postmodern art.

- Icons are made according to the rules of reverse perspective, and in this way they never adopted the attempt to present an illusion of the natural space that we find in post-Renaissance painting, which drew a lot of criticism from postmodern writers.

- Every icon expresses the collective tradition of the Church and not the individual creator. Therefore it is consistent with the postmodernist discourse about the death of the author, as it is argued by such philosophers as Michel Foucault and Roland Barthes. The notion of the 'author' or artist, which is so central in modernist art, is not known in iconography: it is only in post-Byzantine icons that iconographers started signing their works.

- Icons are not made for artistic appreciation but to be used as liturgical objects, and in this way they correspond to the postmodern, post-Warhol demand for the collapse of the limits between art and life. In other words, they do not try to set forth art as a separate reality (as much of modernist art does), but they try to unite the heavenly and the earthly realms.

- Finally, as living images and commentaries of the Bible, icons are not directly affected by the postmodern 'collapse of the big narratives'.

All this indicates that there is something strangely compatible between our age and the sacred art of the East, in all its spiritual aspect. Icons, perhaps more than any other religious expression, have the capability to convey their spiritual message at the level of a (shared) experience. As much as iconography is firmly based on the biblical tradition, it belongs to a tradition that is not content with the sterile recitation or repetition of the text, but it engages it at a deeper level, and it lets this engagement and its spiritual and liturgical significance come through. In a way that touches on the epistemology of theology, icons provide a *sacred topos*, a field where the biblical content, the tradition of the community that wrote it in the first place, the spiritual experience of the medieval mind, and contemporary experience meet.

Far from trying to modernize the message of the Gospel and to re-contextualize it in a way that can bring it closer to our modern experience but perhaps compromise to some extent its spiritual weight, iconography can offer a perspective for the understanding, interpretation and dissemination of the Bible. This may not be easy, but it certainly has the potential to lead the viewer towards a profound, theologically mature, simultaneously simple and complex, reading of the Bible.

Suggested reading

Andreas Andreopoulos, *Metamorphosis: The Transfiguration in Byzantine Theology and Iconography* (Crestwood, NY: SVS Press, 2005).

Gabriel Bunge, *The Rublev Trinity* (Crestwood, NY: SVS Press, 2007).

Anna Kartsonis, *Anastasis: The Making of an Image* (Princeton: Princeton University Press, 1986).

6

The image and the Word:
A chapel dimension

CLYDE BINFIELD

In addition to those Christian denominations for whom visual imagery was central to worship, the Nonconformist chapel tradition also contributed in no small way to the visualization of the biblical word. In this chapter, Clyde Binfield examines the important contribution of the chapel tradition to biblical art and architecture.

Introduction

Contrary to received opinion, the Nonconformist chapel in the nineteenth and twentieth centuries was not at all lacking in biblical imagery but played a significant part in making the biblical story come alive in painting and stained glass. In this chapter, I hope to persuade the reader not to neglect chapel culture in assessing the importance of the visual in communicating and disseminating the biblical message.

The starting point of this study must surely be Amsterdam, that heartland of Calvinistic capitalism, where two great buildings capture the spirit of that city's mercantile supremacy. The first, from the mid seventeenth century, is today the Royal Palace. It was built, however, as the Town Hall and its architect, Jacob van Campen, and its overseeing sculptor, Artus Quellien, combined to create the eighth wonder of the world. Here was a universe of symbolism. No visitor could escape it and none could fail to note that – apart from the High Court, used only for passing the death sentence – the symbolism, though diverse, was wholly classical. Only in the High Court, its bronze doors held shut by the serpent who tempted Eve, was due precedence given to biblical imagery such as the Eye of God, the Last Judgement, and the Judgement of Solomon; and even there the Greek Judgement of Zeleucus and the Roman Judgement of Brutus found a place. Campen's building truly celebrates mercantile magnificence.

The second building, from the end of the nineteenth century, is more rugged and expresses the juggernaut quality of successful commerce. It is Berlage's *Koopmansbeurs* or Stock Exchange. Hendrick-Petrus Berlage (1856–1934) is one of modern Europe's watershed architects who aimed at a truly contemporary style which would celebrate as honestly as possible the prime purpose of architecture, the art of enclosing space. That is the architect's trick, to liberate space by enclosing it. A building is a complex of spaces enclosed by walls. If space is the building's purpose, the wall is its essential element explaining the space which it encloses. The building should be coherent, the decoration of its walls subordinated to what is being explained, hence the bare brick grandeur of Amsterdam's uncompromising Stock Exchange. Berlage liked brick, the natural Dutch building material, for its texture and the power it could give a building. He used it, unmasked, to unite interior and exterior and to convey a message. In effect, his buildings were sermons. This particular building contains a series of murals by Jan Toorop (1858–1928), many of which are inspired by the Bible. One illustrates that most suggestive conversation, Jesus talking to the woman by the well at Sychar, while another illustrates Jesus overturning the tables of the money-changers in the Temple. Those were bold subjects for a stock exchange, art not just as sermon but as socialist sermon for stockbrokers who had already braved panels representing humankind, past, present and future, set above flattened fellow burghers, Calvinists disguised as cornerstones. It is not wholly surprising that Berlage's *Koopmansbeurs* has been turned into an exhibition centre and conference hall. Amsterdam's sermonizing stock exchange is now a talking shop.

Amsterdam serves to remind us of the inescapable, if problematic, link between religion, especially Christianity, and not least its Calvinistic variants, and art, craft and society. The Netherlands was at various times a crossroads of art: a few years after the completion of his Stock Exchange, Berlage found himself excited by artists such as Frank Lloyd Wright and Le Corbusier. The Dutch artist Jan Toorop had met William Morris and would influence Charles Rennie Mackintosh. One might multiply such examples of mutual exchanges. From the next generation the formation of Piet Mondrian (1872–1944), who was as seminal in art as Berlage was in architecture, cannot be fully appreciated without knowledge of his Calvinist origins (his father was a Dutch Reformed Church school headmaster). More famously, there is that Dutch parson's son, Vincent van Gogh (1853–90), whose twenties were a tension between art and religion, both beckoning him professionally, played out in Holland, Belgium, England and France. Van Gogh, Berlage, Toorop, Mondrian, Mackintosh, Lloyd Wright and Le Corbusier spanned two watershed generations in art and architecture. The mindset into which each was born, and from which none wholly escaped, was clearly Reformed.

Van Gogh takes us to England where, for much of 1876, he was in Middlesex lodging with and working for the Slade-Joneses. The evidence suggests that van Gogh and the Slade-Joneses got on very well together. Thomas Slade-Jones was a Congregationalist who kept a boys' school in Isleworth and ministered to a church in Turnham Green, so newly formed that as yet it worshipped in a tin tabernacle. Van Gogh also had contacts with local Wesleyans for whom one Sunday he preached a sermon, the text of which still survives. Its theme was a pilgrim's progress and its inevitable association, on which the preacher naturally played, was with Bunyan's *Pilgrim's Progress*; but at its heart, illuminated by a poem of Christina Rossetti's, was a generalized account of a Pre-Raphaelite-ish painting, recently exhibited, which has since been identified as *God Speed! Pilgrims Setting out for Canterbury: Time of Chaucer.* Bunyan's pilgrim was more appropriate than Chaucer's pilgrims for Wesleyan and Congregational Sunday hearers, but a painting would have struck none of them as an improper illustration for a sermon and, whether or not they recognized this particular painting, they would certainly have seen illustrated, or even exhibited, plenty like it. The young Dutchman was thus tapping into a shared experience of visual biblical culture.

Thomas Slade-Jones was an admirable pastor–teacher from a relatively assured small-town background, while his wife, Annie, came from an enviably circumstanced northern background and belonged to a nationwide connection of ministerial, professional, commercial, and literary Congregationalists for whom art was a natural accessory. Turnham Green was a strategic setting for his church since it happened to be close to Bedford Park, that pioneer garden suburb where artists and writers lived hugger-mugger with solicitors and stockbrokers. It was also only a brisk walk away from Hammersmith Mall, where George Macdonald lived for several years, where William Morris developed his socialist ideas, and where Thomas Cobden-Sanderson formed his Doves Bindery. These were suggestive names for cultivated Dissenters: indeed, all were part of the same culturally evolving society. It may have been an increasingly complex society, and it is certainly important to understand the distinctions and gradations within it, but we should beware of over-compartmentalization. When Turnham Green's Congregationalists replaced their tin tabernacle with a stone church they turned to an accomplished Congregational architect, Lewis Banks, whose circle included another accomplished Congregational architect, John Sulman, who had entered the original competition that resulted in Berlage's *Koopmansbeurs*.

The Victorian Dissenters

When we focus on who and what Victorian Dissenters were, we are looking at one or more of three types: ministers, lay leadership, and the rank and file. The ministers (and their wives) constituted their prime social lightning conductors and were their intelligentsia; the lay leaders tended to be successful men, upwardly mobile, vulnerable no doubt to the trappings of status, but certainly open to the possibilities (and allurements) of education and to the enlarged opportunities for cultural growth in all its fullness. Spiritual, intellectual and aesthetic discovery and fulfilment were quite as much a duty (and true pleasure) as the confirmation and announcement of status or respectability. The Dissenting rank and file encompassed adherents as well as members and were of both sexes and all ages. All, quite consciously, were at the social and spiritual cutting edge. While some dissented from social convenience, others dissented from social awkwardness. All, by virtue of their dissent, were in some sense at odds with what was generally deemed normal, even if they were announcing what ought to be normal in an ideal world. Their dissent, therefore, involved a stand. It is quite significant, too, that so many Dissenters came from what might be called the mental art-workers of society: compositors, type-setters, printers, lithographers, engravers, journalists, newspapermen, booksellers, publishers, arts-and-craftsmen moving towards the professions, cultural mediators and popularizers in word, music and picture. Indeed, no part of English religious society was free from their influence.

That there were tensions goes without saying: tensions that were as old as organized religion, defined by theology and churchmanship and entrenched by social constraints. For chapel could stifle and expel art as well as liberate it. Chapel represented a cast of mind opposed to counterfeit, and what was art if not counterfeit? Nevertheless, from the 1840s and gathering exponential force in each succeeding decade, chapel blazed in colour and texture, in stone, wood and glass, in symbol and picture, and across the pages of Scripture and tract. In all these ways chapel spoke. It could do no other for people of the Word. For chapel imaged the Bible and was focused on the Word. As a structure, chapel was a machine for communicating the Word, as a concept the church or society which gathered in a chapel was a community, a way of life, for embodying the Word. In sermon, reading and exposition, in prayer and song, the Word was the focus. Pulpit, desk, galleries, pews, table, baptistery, demonstrated that. A chapel's power is still best felt from what is now usually its least frequented part, the back gallery. From there the rhythm of pews sweeps insistently towards a pulpit less raised above contradiction than poised to reach the furthest corner, rather as the Great White Pulpit of London's City Temple reached to the Rockies, as they nicknamed the distant top gallery of that world-famous, world-embracing church. Any chapel that was fit for purpose was a theatre for the drama of eternity.

Far from London, on Wadsworth Moor in Yorkshire's West Riding, is Wainsgate Baptist Chapel, now in the care of the Historic Chapels Trust, where a church was gathered between 1750 and 2001. The present building, solid against the hillside, was opened in May 1860. Its exterior betrays no hint of ecclesiastical fashion or ecclesiological revolution. In 1891, however, the interior was modernized: yet, even though the organ, pulpit, platform, the choir arrangements, pews and windows were replaced, it remains unmistakably a chapel. But how discordant were some of the changes that were made? This was clearly signalled from the first: in the opulence of the door's glass handles and the lilies etched in its glass; in the oak communion rail with its base of primroses, its supports of vine and fruit, its top of leaves and acorns, profusely carved to protect the baptistery; and a table and chairs such as might grace a fine dining room. In addition, the Word was now to be spoken from a wonderland pulpit made of alabaster, Genoan green marble, Numidian red marble, rouge red marble, Mexican onyx, and Californian jasper, with three Carrara panels, *The Baptism of Christ*, *The Agony in the Garden* and *The*

Blessing of the Bread and Wine, wordlessly conveying Word and Sacrament, however wordy the pulpit's occupant. From Word spoken to Word sung, the organist was as powerfully placed as the preacher, his choir to hand, warmed and furnished with careful flexibility. There should now have been little to distract the attention from the heart of Wainsgate worship but, were the eye to wander, it was bound to rest on three colourful windows depicting the Way of the Cross, the Crucifixion, and the Resurrection, rich in traditional colour and design.

What is memorably conserved at Wainsgate is a natural response to opportunity: door handles can be useful, it helps to have a choir suitably positioned, and why should people who know their Bible not see as well as hear its best expression when they worship? The Gospel scenes in Carrara marble and painted glass are no afterthought: they are integral to Wainsgate's ecclesiology, and the chapel's survival is to be treasured as representative of chapel culture, not unique. So what particularly eased the introduction of glass and marble to image the Bible in these mills for communicating words and Word, filled and operated by mental art-workers? The answer brings us back to the importance of setting and ministry, and three specific examples (two Congregational and one Baptist) will illustrate the ecclesiastical trends and viewpoints that enabled art works to play a more significant role in chapel culture.

Three influential preachers

Henry Allon

Henry Allon (1818–92) ministered at Union Chapel, Islington, from 1844 to 1892. In 1867, he preached on 'The Glory of the Sanctuary'. His sermon was a masterpiece of care and emphasized the essence of congregational worship:

To a mere observer of outward things it is but an ordinary assembly of men and women. Simple words are uttered, spiritual truths are set forth, the appeal is solely to intellectual conception and to religious consciousness. Our worship depends upon neither consecrated place nor ordained priest, only upon what we ourselves are and feel in God's spiritual presence.[1]

However, Allon balanced the individual – our worship is 'the direct spiritual communion with God of each individual heart' – with the communal, and argued for the place of ornament and art in the chapel:

If there be waste in the precious ointment which love lavishes, is there not something worse than waste in the demur which is made to it? What love is worthy that is not lavish in its offer-ings? . . . If our love build a house for God . . . should not its adornments have some congruity with the wealth and social habits of those who build it?[2]

Peter Taylor Forsyth

Just over 20 years later, those sentiments were more rigorously echoed by Peter Taylor Forsyth (1848–1921), who initially worked in Hackney in London but later settled in a newly built Congregational church in Leicester. His first published work was a collection of children's addresses, *Pulpit Parables for Young Hearers* (1886). One of them, 'Baby Babble', is at first reading a quintessential Victorian sermonette. It expounds Psalm 8.2 ('Out of the mouths of babes and sucklings hast thou ordained strength . . .') to which is appended the exposition of a poem 'by a very great and wise man'. The language, however, is part fairy-tale, part stained-glass window and part painting (reminiscent of a blend of medieval Italian, primitive Dutch pastoral and Pre-Raphaelite sentiment). Forsyth's young Hackney hearers would have been familiar with the National Gallery in London – thus the genius of expounding a psalm, recreated in a Congregational pulpit, in the language of the Old Masters:

Once on a time, long, long ago, there lived in the country a good man, who, before he went to bed, used to go out and sit in the porch of his house to think in silence about God. One night, before going out of doors, he looked at his wife and his children, and saw his baby crowing, and smiling, and talking words not to be written by any pen in the world. And as he looked his heart was softened, and the father became himself, for the time, like a little child; and he forgot the hard battles that he had to fight in the world all day, and he felt kindly to everybody. And he heard, as it were, the voice of God speaking with a sweet power in the babble of his baby on its mother's breast, as you might hear the solemn whisper of God in the prattle of a brook that runs through deep meadow land. And the mother's face hung over her child like a happy mood, and her black hair was like high heaven's dark blue, and her eyes were like stars in a twilight night. Then he went out of doors. And when he lifted up his gaze, lo, there was not a cloud to be seen, and it seemed as if it were neither dark nor light. It was like daylight without the sun, or like midnight without the dark. For above him was the great, round moon, and a family of little stars such as no man could number were shining upon the blue floor of heaven which no man can measure. And away upon the fields that ran to the distant hills were scattered the dwellings of other men, with mothers and children, and the stalls of cattle, and the folds of sheep. And there flowed the river, with the sleeping fish, beneath the stones, and far, far away was the sea with the great rocking ships and plunging whales. And the heart of this man was filled and lifted up. The moonlight, flooding the sky, and gilding the fields, and white on the silent river, was like the glory of God which covers all things, and gives them peace. And he was so full of solemn joy, of hearts and babes, of men and their mothers, of heaven and its God, that he could not be silent, so he broke out into this eighth Psalm, which is a hymn of praise.[3]

Forsyth's fluently concentrated word painting for Hackney's St Thomas's Square Congregationalists is not so far removed in time or spirit from Vincent van Gogh's halting essay for Richmond's Kew Road Wesleyans. The painterly tone of his pulpit parable gains in significance when it is recalled that Forsyth's next book was *Religion in Recent Art being Expository Lectures on Rosetti, Burne Jones, Watts, Holman Hunt, and Wagner* (1889). These lectures, which Forsyth described as 'lay sermons', were delivered to Charles Rowley's Ancoats Brotherhood. They were 'residuary products of the unique Art Collection in the late Manchester Exhibition', and although they were the product of Forsyth's theologically liberal years (and Rowley, an art dealer with a social conscience, was innocent of any theological orthodoxy), their theme remained an abiding interest of Forsyth's, rekindled in *Christ on Parnassus: Lectures on Art, Ethic, and Theology* (1911). He was convinced that 'the National Gallery represents an interest as integral to the church in its own way as the national Parliament'.

Alexander McLaren

From 1858 to 1903 Union Chapel, Manchester, was the setting for the ministry of Alexander McLaren (1826–1910). It housed one of Manchester's most powerful congregations and McLaren was one of Britain's most influential Baptist ministers. In 1863, accompanied by his wife, her sister and an art-collecting Union deacon, McLaren spent some weeks in Italy. These provided the inspiration for his lectures for Union's Young Men's Society which he published as *A Spring Holiday in Italy* – his equivalent, as he disarmingly put it, of the 'little, dingy photographs of great pictures' which tourists habitually bring home. In San Pietro in Vincoli, Rome (see Figure 8, p. 79), McLaren came face to face with a masterpiece by 'the greatest of the Italians next to Dante'. He recaptured it for Union's young men:

> We lift the hanging mat, leathern bordered and greasy, and enter the cool nave. A long range of Doric pillars divides it from the aisles. Between them we catch a glimpse of a solemn figure seated in a marble niche against one side-wall. When we come nearer a strange awe creeps over us as if the thing were a living soul looking out from the stone. It is Michael Angelo's great statue of Moses, which, like all works of high and earnest imagination, can be caricatured by shallow people, and cannot be understood nor felt unless approached in some sense in the same spirit in which they were created. Sitting there, with one leg bent backwards from the knee, one mighty arm, with iron muscles and great veins, thrust into the heavy coils of a beard that flows in torrents down the broad chest; the other hand grasping the upper edge of the strong tables, the kingly head turned slightly to gaze with looks of high command on 'the many thousands of Israel', the autocratic mouth parting, as if to roll forth 'Thus saith the Lord', and stamped with traces of sorrow and opposition, the massive nostrils wide distended with conscious power, the deep-sunk eye ready to flash out its lightnings from beneath the cloud-caves of the thunderous eyebrows, the forehead knotted by the energy of will of the awful spirit within, and the strong locks shaped into the hint of the traditional horns, the emblem of power and rule – this tremendous figure lives for ever in the memory, as a person girt with all the attributes of a true king of men, the leader and lawgiver, the organ for the voice of God. Stern and inflexible, he is the very spirit of that ancient Law. These vehement hands were fit to grasp without trembling the outstretched rod that

brought the sea over Pharaoh's host: that furrowed brow could well dominate and quell the cowardly slaves whom he lifted into a nation. These deep eyes are purged to behold the glories of the Divine presence within the cloud; and no wonder that such a face, all aflame with the brightness of God, had to veil its awful radiance when it came amongst common men.
The thought that guided the impetuous pen of the apostle has guided the impetuous chisel of the sculptor, and the work of the one is a noble commentary on the words of the other. 'The ministration of death written and engraved in stones was glorious so that the children of Israel could not steadfastly behold the face of Moses for the glory of his countenance.' I know no work of sculpture that thrills one with such a sublime sense of power, and with such an unnameable apocalypse of a spiritual presence in the material vehicle, as that awful lawgiver sitting there in the long aisle of the quiet church . . . No man that ever wrought with chisel or brush has smitten with such sense and strong hand the deepest chords of my soul as he whom I venture to believe, with Mr Ruskin, 'the greatest mind that art ever inspired', Michael Angelo Buonarroti.[4]

That suggestive gloss on verbal inspiration was echoed with brisk economy 20 years later by a Baptist-educated Congregationalist, Henry Bond, a young Cambridge lawyer. Bond's aesthetic tastes were commendably up-to-date: Botticelli, newly reclaimed from oblivion, Andrea del Sarto, Raphael, Fra Angelico and Giotto, among many others. He too was struck by Moses.

It impresses one immensely if one keeps in mind that he is looking down upon the Israelites, playing the fool in some way, and trying to keep his disgust and indignation from breaking out. It is certainly one of the most impressive sculptures I ever saw.

As Allon explained and McLaren and Forsyth demonstrated, there was nothing passive about word-dominated worship. It explored and evoked a disciplined but imaginative response consonant with the Christian life, which was itself an imaging of God. 'Art is human nature', ran Edmund Burke's epigraph to Forsyth's *Religion in Art*. Whether 'Christian' or not, art, for Christians, need not be counterfeit.

How representative were Henry Allon, Henry Bond, Peter Taylor Forsyth and Alexander McLaren? They were certainly representative of rising men: Allon a builder's son, Forsyth a postman's, Bond a wholesale grocer's son, McLaren a merchant's. Their interests and connections ranged nationwide. Allon and Forsyth were men whose social position, intellectual grasp and consequent influence had been confirmed and enlarged by their call to ministry, while Henry Bond was the prime mover behind the prominent rebuilding of Cambridge's Congregational Church.

Bond's Cambridge Congregational Church had a powerful focal point, a six-sided apse guarded by a bold stone pulpit. A master text ran round the apse in Rust's mosaic: 'Thine, O Lord, is the greatness, and the power, and the glory, and the majesty' (1 Chronicles 29.11). The six lancet windows of its three middle sides incorporated local stained glass 'comprising single figures and small groups from Scripture history', while the wood-panelled, domical ceiling was to feature a 'series of subjects suggested by Psalm 148'. Whether from economy or conservatism, those subjects were not, in fact, featured and in 1907 the lancet figures and groups from Scripture history were replaced by figures from Congregational history, Milton and Cromwell among them. These were executed by Morris and Company in memory of Henry Bond's father. Had the Bible been downgraded? Or had a more constitutional ecclesiastical balance been achieved between Congregationalism's fourfold use of the Bible, tradition, reason and conscience, expressed in this new building's text, windows, pulpit and pews, and indicative of further distinctive aesthetic development?

The contribution of Frederic Shields (1833–1911)

It is here that Frederic Shields (1833–1911), artist and agonized man-in-the-pew, provides a curiously apt case study, sometimes described as 'Manchester's Pre-Raphaelite'. His reputation has suffered physically and critically: while his culminating work has been destroyed, his early work has been dismissed as bland and sentimental and his later, religious, work as cold and austere. His religious views have doubtlessly mystified, perhaps repelled, those whose interest might otherwise have been aroused by his unusual domestic circumstances. Nonetheless, as metal art-worker turned artist, as Calvinist struggling to express his art as fulfilment of his Christian vocation, and as unique in personality as he was representative in style, development and professional success, he illuminates what chapel attempted to image at this particular time (Figure 10).

Shields secured the affectionate epistolary respect of Charles Kingsley, John Ruskin, G. F. Watts and Holman Hunt, and the lasting friendship of Dante Gabriel Rossetti, Ford Madox Brown and Charles Rowley, the art-dealer. Alfred Waterhouse, the architect, was an invaluable mediator of influential patronage and Shields tended to keep the loyalty of his patrons. Significant influences in his work include his upbringing, the chapel dimension and its developing relationship to his art.

Shields's scant early education included time spent at a charity school followed by drawing classes at a Mechanics' Institute, more classes at Somerset House, daily draughtsmanship at the British Museum, and posts as a lithographer in London and the north. Lithography was a precarious trade and the firms for which Shields worked seldom survived.

Religion and its relationship to art were consistent threads in Shields's life. The schoolboy who wrote down the text and theme of each Sunday's sermon was the compulsive sketcher who 'revelled in gleaners and milkmaids, and rustic lovers, and a box of colours for the

Figure 10: Reproduction of Frederic Shields's painting *Lord Save Me*.
Ceredigion Museum.

first time'. The eldest son who urged his brother Edwin 'not to neglect God's Word as he valued God's favour' and begged him to avoid current literature and its 'cheap compounds of trashy novels, broad grins, and comic songs', was the young artist whose first exhibited work reminded a Manchester reviewer 'of the manner of Rubens' and for whom Ford Madox Brown's *Christ Washing Peter's Feet* was a revelation when encountered at Manchester's Art Treasures Exhibition.

Shields eventually attracted wider attention – particularly his 60 designs for *Pilgrim's Progress* (1859) and a similar series for Defoe's *Plagues of London* (1863). They demanded meticulous accuracy. *Pilgrim's Progress*, he reflected, presented 'a mighty drama, its scene thinly veiling the invisible world . . . Now, at last, my life, I felt, had begun.' In 1864 Shields met A. J. Scott (1805–66), Manchester's 'Nestor of heretics', the dissident Presbyterian minister turned university professor. But Scott was also at the heart of a theologically broad literary circle, his friendships with men like Thomas Erskine of Linlathen and George Macdonald were shared by several who later became Shields's patrons, and Manchester was alive with patrons. Those who came his way were religiously varied. The calico printer Frederick Craven (1818–94), for example, was a Unitarian. Particular mention, however, might be made of William Graham (1816–85), whose collection of Italian Old Masters and Pre-Raphaelites was famous. When he was in Lancashire he worshipped at Alexander McLaren's Union Chapel; when he was in London he worshipped at Samuel Martin's Congregational Westminster Chapel.

McLaren was impressed with Shields's work and responded to photographs of windows which Shields had designed for a Lancashire industrialist's Scottish chapel:

In power and harmony, in weighty meaning expressed in fair shape, in delightful and not too misty symbolism, they seem to me to surpass all that you have done, so far as I know it. And one feels that they are not the work of a man who looks at Christ as an artist, but of a painter who looks at him as a Christian. I only wish they were not going to be buried in a hole in Ayrshire, where nobody will see them but Presbyterians, who will think them 'Rags of the whore of Babylon', or spinners who will wonder what they cost . . .[5]

Ten years after that, McLaren commented on a lunette which Shields had designed for a hotbed of Anglo-Catholicism, St Barnabas, Pimlico:

Surely you are meant to be the painter of true sacred subjects. The old men had a very narrow range of these: annunciations, crucifixions, resurrections, ascensions, last suppers, are about all, barring the cartoons. Oh, there's the woman taken in adultery, too, for the sake of the opportunity of painting some Italian harlot, and then there's no more. You have faith and imagination and mysticism, and you can draw, so I hope that you will have strength to make more of the gospel stories live to us . . .[6]

In 1898 McLaren wrote to Shields, complimenting him on his portrait of St Paul:

Your noble 'Paul' (what do you call him saint for?) I think you have never done a truer embodiment of a great soul. The wasted eagerness, the weakness reinforced by supernatural strength, are magnificently rendered. I wish every lazy, smooth-haired and smooth-souled preacher had a copy of it hanging in his 'study' to flame down rebukes at him. I have had him framed to hang in mine, and you, through him, will spur me often.[7]

The consistent threat of Baptist art-criticism reached Shields at the climax of his religious and professional career. Back in January 1865, about the time that Shields and McLaren first met, another new friend, Dante Gabriel Rossetti, asked Shields if he would furnish stained-glass designs for 'a firm with which I am connected (Messrs. Morris, Marshall, Faulkner & Co)'. Shields had replied that it was not really in his line – but, in fact, the increasingly ambitious schemes with which he became associated included stained-glass designs. Close upon each other, thanks chiefly to the good offices of Alfred Waterhouse, came commissions for six frescoes for Manchester Town Hall (not in fact executed), windows on 'The Triumph of Faith' for Sir William Houldsworth's chapel near Kilmarnock, and windows and mosaics for the Duke of Westminster's chapel at Eaton Hall. The vocation which began with *Pilgrim's Progress* approached its peak with the Duke's *Te Deum*:

> The opportunity for which my whole longings and aims had
> fitted me come at last – late – but come! My soul kindled and
> flamed with the subject accepted, the glorious hymn of St
> Ambrose, the *Te Deum*. Nearly ninety subjects, all told, not
> isolated but such as could be linked in blessed continuity – to
> keep the heart hot, and the mind quick, with its grand
> purpose – the praise of God and of His Son Jesus Christ, from
> the lives of apostles, prophets, martyrs, and the Holy Church
> of all the ages. My love of the written word of God and all my
> longings after nobler avenues for expression in my Art has
> been fitting me for such a work.[8]

Shields mused on the technical challenges, the 'fine disposition of drapery' for example, which only Fra Angelico had perfected. He also mused on the 'glass, usually fixed in churches' and his own duty to express his art 'subject to the authority of the Scriptures':

It is my aim to make the designs as distinctly didactic as possible, without losing regard to the necessity of decorative effect. And in style I am always struggling after purity of contour, elevation of individual character and intensity of expression. Yes, it is only stained glass, an art invented by Goths and only fit to be continued by Goths in my esteem; but it finds me noblest matter of design, keeps me germinating high thoughts and inventions, and lifts me out of the petty trifling of petty subjects and imitative facility to which I must otherwise have gone on applying my efforts.[9]

Later critics regretted the impact on his art of such firm high-mindedness, but could there be a more Nonconformist apologia or a clearer insight as to how first the Scriptures and then the Church and then the ongoing march of faith, literal interpretation and corresponding accuracy competing with vision and personality, came to be imaged in Nonconformist churches? And Shields's greatest test and fullest opportunity had yet to come.

By the late 1870s he was moving in the most elevated and serious circles. Thus he met his last and most representative patron, Mrs Russell Gurney (1823–96), who came from an impeccable Evangelical background and was also widely admired as an educationist and feminist. As the wife and widow of a universally well-regarded Conservative MP she was a prominent patron of many causes, but she had one personal cause in particular: a memorial to her husband. Beginning simply as a decorated room, it then turned into a chapel of rest, a Puritan Sistine Chapel in miniature, housing a pictorial programme of Christian art. Shields was to be its artist. 'I tremble with desire and fear towards the work . . .' he wrote in 1887, 'it involves great issues, and may lead to a new departure in the alliance or service of Art to Piety. Symbols affect men's imagination and faith mightily still.'

By late 1888 they had a site and an architect. The site, near Marble Arch, was a largely disused mortuary chapel on Bayswater Road, belonging to St George's, Hanover Square. The architect, Herbert Horne (1864–1916), was a young aesthete still in his twenties. The evolution and completion of their Chapel of the Ascension (Russell Gurney had died on Ascension Day) was fraught with difficulties. Mrs Russell Gurney lived to see it opened but it took another 14 years and a Chancery suit to see it properly completed. Horne and Shields travelled to Italy to savour the choicest examples of Lombardic architecture, 'so simple and pure'. Horne was seized by Pietrasanta's *Santa Maria della Grazie*. Shields found that Italian faces stirred him almost more than Italian buildings, but the nobility of theme took priority as he sought to develop a sequence of ideas, illustrated by wealth of figurative ideas and symbols and types.

> To give the spirit of the Revelation of God to man – from the beginning – conveyed in the forms of Scripture translated as much as may be into the shapes at art's command. To glorify the Father by a good work which shall teach, admonish, and accentuate, with the never silent speech of Art.[10]

Shields described the chapel as 'an Arena Capella to myself: Prophets and Apostles, Christian virtues and worldly vices, Gospel and Apostolic history, types and symbols all enter into it . . .' And he firmly told young Horne that his 'paintings are not for the building, but the building for the paintings'.

Did it work? Was it any fitter for purpose, say, than Berlage's *Koopmansbeurs*? Apparently not. Arthur Porritt, who prevailed on Shields to show him round this temple of 'art in the spirit of English Evangelicalism', recalled that it was 'sadly unappreciated', and eventually licensed (against Shields's wish) for Anglican services. And it was allowed no chance to grow in the affections of posterity because it was largely destroyed in 1940 and finally demolished in 1969. Surviving photographs, however, certainly stir interest in the project's scope and in the nature of the partnership between the Broad Church patroness, the Evangelical artist and the aesthete architect. The fate of Shields's *Te Deum* tends to confirm Forsyth's comment that 'bald devotion and trivial art are alike symptoms of that spiritual poverty which underlies the hard-featured piety of our pushing Christian type'. It should not, however, obscure their significance in the development of a mindset which believed that it could and should image the Word, picture the tradition, and keep faith with the Church that is the body of Christ.

Conclusion

It is clear from this brief overview of Nonconformist movements and culture in the nineteenth century that, although there was no uniform pattern, many individuals were very favourably disposed towards the idea of 'visualizing' important episodes from the Bible. Since many Dissenters were also 'art-workers' by profession (printers, engravers and lithographers), it was only natural that they should extend their interest in art to their places of worship. Those who adorned the chapels in nineteenth- and twentieth-century Britain believed that even though the biblical Word was central to the deepening of their faith, the visual expression of that Word could be equally illuminating and inspiring.

Notes

1 W. H. Harwood, *Henry Allon: Pastor and Teacher* (London, 1894), p. 128.
2 Harwood, *Henry Allon*, p. 119.
3 P. T. Forsyth, *Pulpit Parables for Young Hearers* (Manchester, 1886), pp. 186–7.
4 E. T. McLaren, *Dr. McLaren of Manchester: A Sketch* (London, 1911), p. 94.

5 E. Mills, *The Life and Letters of Frederic Shields* (London, 1912), p. 239.

6 Mills, *Life and Letters*, p. 299.

7 Mills, *Life and Letters*, p. 331.

8 Mills, *Life and Letters*, p. 229.

9 Mills, *Life and Letters*, p. 229.

10 Mills, *Life and Letters*, p. 305.

Suggested reading

John Harvey, *The Art of Piety* (Cardiff: University of Wales Press, 1995).

Anthony Jones, *Welsh Chapels* (Stroud/Cardiff: Alan Sutton/National Museum of Wales, 1996).

D. Ben Rees, *Chapels in the Valleys* (Upton: Ffynnon Press, 1975).

7

Visual typology and Pentecostal theology: The paintings of Nicholas Evans

JOHN HARVEY

The work of the twentieth-century Welsh artist Nicholas Evans illustrates how art could be significantly influenced by a particular theological mindset, in this case by Pentecostal theology. John Harvey explores, through the work of Nicholas Evans, how art could be regarded as having a spiritual essence and utility. For Evans, art was a means of communion with God, and a hymn of praise and adoration. His sense of the divine was also experienced in the very act of making the picture. He believed that he was aided in the act by a power outside himself.

Introduction

In his *Summa Theologica*, the medieval exegete Thomas Aquinas (c. 1225–74) defined four senses of Holy Scripture: the literal, the allegorical, the moral and the analogical. The literal sense is the literal or evident meaning of the words, as understood according to the genre of the text; the allegorical sense often implied the text's Christological meaning – the way in which (when apprehended by faith) Scripture speaks, through symbol, simile and metaphor, of Christ; the moral or tropological sense is the meaning the text has in relation to the conduct of the members of Christ – how it transforms their hearts and minds and structures their behaviour in accordance with the principles and commandments of the Bible; while the analogical or eschatological sense is the meaning that the text has in relation to doctrines of the end time and the believer's supernatural hope of heaven. This approach to biblical interpretation was (although sometimes ill-conceived and fanciful in its application) derived from the theology of types or typology. Typology represents an early Christian method of cross-correspondence between the Jewish and Christian Scriptures which establishes continuities between people, things and events in the Old Testament (called types) and people, things and events in the New Testament (known as anti-types). The former (the type) foreshadows the latter (the anti-type, also referred to as the 'true'). Types are biblical. For example, Christ spoke of his physical elevation at the Crucifixion as having been prefigured by Moses setting up on a pole the brazen serpent, which healed those who had been bitten by a snake and who looked at it (John 3.14). Earlier in the history of biblical exposition the Alexandrian scholar Origen (185–254 CE) believed that typological relationships were not confined to the Judeo-Christian Scriptures; the whole universe is, he conceived, pervaded with symbols and types (or patterns) of the invisible or supernatural world. Everything that existed was not only a thing in itself but also a shadow of something else. Thus, everything had a double aspect: one aspect was corporeal and sensible, the other spiritual and invisible.

Mining and religion: the double aspect

This principle of the 'double aspect' can be applied to the exegesis not only of the Scriptures but of pictures. Semioticians (most notably Roland Barthes (1915–80)) have argued that some visual images possess ambivalence, that is to say, a double valency or twin powers that are mutually interactive and interdependent. An ambivalent image may be conceived as having an upper and lower storey: the lower storey is the realm of the visible, ostensible, evident and denoted subject of the picture; the upper storey, of the implied, connoted or evoked subject of the picture. One image: two storeys. Two storeys: two stories. The paintings of Welsh artist Nicholas Evans (1907–2004) comprise two stories: one about mining, the other about religion. These two stories are often told together. At one and the same time they speak of the things of earth and heaven, life and death, the temporal and the eternal, the flesh and the spirit, and coal and the soul. Mining belongs to the lower storey: it is the visible, physical, denoted and evident subject of his paintings. Religion belongs to the upper storey: it is the invisible, spiritual, implied and connoted subject of the paintings. This chapter draws attention to several ways in which his depiction of coalmining summons biblical and religious concepts, and also to how Evans's Pentecostal mindset contributed to his understanding of the origin and nature and his gift and work.

Evans was, for only two years of his life, a pitboy in a colliery in Aberdare near Glamorgan in Wales. When he was 16 years old, he left the pit to become a railwayman and a lay-preacher in the Pentecostal Church. Evans's practice as a painter began in the 1970s, on his retirement, and continued for a quarter of a century, over a period that saw the terminal decline of the South Wales coal industry. In the 1980s, the Conservative government's determination to reduce drastically the size of the coal industry forced the National Union of Mineworkers into a year-long and, ultimately, doomed strike in 1984. Evans's paintings do not convey an overt political response to that context of the coal crisis. Evans was essentially a history painter rather than a commentator on contemporary times. The nearest he came to depicting the time in which he lived was in representing the disaster at the Pantglas Junior School, Aberfan, Glamorgan in 1966 – nearly a decade before he began painting – when a spoil heap slid on to the village, killing 144 people, 116 of them children. Nevertheless, his work provides a salutary pictorial backdrop to the end of mining in Wales – a visual vestige, conserving a memory (that extended far beyond the recollection of anyone alive) of what was being lost and suffered. The paintings show scenes not only of the means of production but also of the culture and community it shaped and with whose fortunes it was inseparably bound up. His representations of lockouts and strike marches, soup kitchens and destitution, were a timely reminder that history repeats itself and, more particularly, of the cycle of suffering that was the habitual lot of the coalminer. Evans's work is, furthermore, a testament to the gruelling conditions and crippling confinement endured by the colliers underground, and to their equally primitive domestic life. He contrasts the miners' bestialization by outward circumstances with scenes of their cultivated inner life. They are shown (during times of religious revival) humbled and enriched by their piety as they gather as congregations below ground, bowed low not by the height of the pit roof but by a contrite heart.

Besides the confrontations between the workers and owners of coal, Evans recalls the miner's lot from life to death, and beyond. *Ashes to Ashes* (1978) depicts the mass interment of miners killed in one of the numerous and horrific colliery disasters in South Wales. The companion piece, *'The Trumpet Shall Sound' – Resurrection* (1979), is also set in a cemetery (Plate 9). However, in contrast, we see not the bodies of miners being lowered into the earth but their souls rising to heaven on the Last Day. In *'The Trumpet Shall Sound'* the lower and the higher realms intersect in the evident or denoted subject. The backdrop (the lower storey) to the scene of multiple ascension includes topographic references to specific places in Aberdare: notably, the local cemetery and parish church, which are brought together as a composite in a manner that cannot be experienced in real life. The rising spirits of the redeemed, each carrying a palm branch, have an ethereal form and rhythmic sway reminiscent (suitably so, given Evans's theology) of the manner in which the tongues of fire that descended on the disciples at Pentecost (Acts

2.1–21) are often represented in medieval painting. The setting for the Resurrection is – as in, for example, Stanley Spencer's (1891–1959) painting *Cookham Resurrection* (1923–7) – the artist's native environment. In contrast to Evans's vision, Spencer's visualization emphasizes the physical resuscitation and individuality of those who have died in Christ. Evans's conception of the resurrected as an anonymous, numerous and numinous flock reflects their transformation into a state of incorruptibility at the last trump.

Biblical and religious evocation: visual typology

This painting, together with the others by Evans mentioned so far, illustrates a story about coalmining. In this respect, Evans's paintings are like the work of other coalminers-turned-artists who have documented the life and times of their industry, providing corroborating insights into the social conditions, technology and dangers of mining from the perspective of insiders. But their pictures occupy only the lower storey: they are earthbound. Evans's work inhabits both storeys (earth and heaven) simultaneously by virtue of visual typology. Like biblical typology, visual typology establishes connections between one thing and another – in the case of Evans's work, between mining images and biblical and religious concepts. These paintings connect the upper and lower storeys in a number of ways, by means of: (1) the paintings' titles; (2) aspects of the formal properties of the work; (3) certain compositional affinities between the scenes of mining and of religious art; and (4) four (often interrelated) approaches to engaging biblical themes, doctrines and concepts (either covertly or explicitly) – (a) biblical allusion; (b) biblical conflation; (c) biblical illustration; and (d) biblical transposition.

The relation of title to image in Evans's paintings follows traditional categorizations for the most part. They can be: descriptive; anecdotal or narrative; and referential. Under the class of descriptive titles we could include *Strike – Gleaners on Slag Tip*. Anecdotal titles include *The Broken Rope*, where the title suggests a story, in this case, the cause of a terrible scene of mutilation. The rope that hauls the coal drams to the surface has snapped. As a consequence, the drams have gone into free fall and crashed into the miners working below. *'The Trumpet Shall Sound' – Resurrection* is an example of a referential title, which refers to a biblical text (1 Corinthians 15.52). There is a further category of title relevant in Evans's work – what the art historian Ernst Gombrich called a 'mood-setter' – which helps to create a portentous or quasi-religious ethos around a work.[1] The title *The Last Bond* falls into this category (Plate 10). It suggests a *double-entendre*. In mining terminology the term 'bond', in its technical sense, is a synonym for the cage that confines the miners and carries them down the pit shaft. However, the meanings one normally associates with the word include imprisonment, slavery and binding together. These emotive overtones invest the title (and, in turn, the image) with other nuances of meaning. 'Bond' evokes the additional sense of the common humanity, circumstance and outlook that unites these miners, a solidarity endorsed by the uniformity with which Evans has portrayed their facial expressions. In this way the image transcends the mere description of an aspect of mining history (to rise above the lower storey). The prefix 'last' indicates the approaching termination of this association. However, the relation of the title to the cause is as indeterminate as the title to the image is enigmatic. (We are free to speculate as to what will bring the solidarity of these miners to an end, whether redundancy or an impending colliery disaster.) The title operates as text, one which identifies and describes the denoted scene (the subject of mining) and, in the instance of *The Last Bond*, connotes a subject in the upper storey too – an intimation of mortality.

However, it is not the title alone that gives rise to the evocation. The title collaborates with certain of the formal properties of the work – that is, the stylistic and representational attributes. The miners' faces are like skulls: eyes are sunken and closed, and the contours of the bone structure sharply defined by the dark shadows of coal-dust on their faces. The rows upon rows of colliers' skull-like heads boxed into the confines of the cage resemble arrangements of skulls found in ossuaries or charnel houses. Evans has conflated the image of the skeleton, the traditional symbol for a *vanitas* and *memento mori* (the inevitability of death), with the representation of the miners. They bear the image and reminder of their own mortality in themselves. The appearance of putrescence implied by the black patches of the coal-dust smeared on their flesh turn the colliers into a kind of half-living, half-dead humanity, suggesting a comparison with images of the medieval *transi* – the grim reaper.

The miners' skull-like faces and skeletal forms suggest an aesthetic for portraying humans significantly at odds with the ideals of classical figure representation typified, for example, by the labourers in the Pre-Raphaelite Ford Madox Brown's (1821–93) painting *Work* (1852–63). Brown depicts the labourer with a noble and heroic form derived from antique sculptures. The painting portrays an ideal conception of manliness, perfect in surface and proportion, his skin and clothes unsullied by the earth and grime of his occupation. Evans's half-naked miners working underground appear disfigured and defiled. In terms of the classical aesthetic, these men are not endowed with nobility, greatness, grace or elegance, but instead are shown in a condition of weakness and vulnerability. The deformation of their bodies may be thought of not only as denoting the ravages of brutal physical labour but also as connoting an externalization of the miners' (and, as we shall see later, metaphorically, of humankind's) natural spiritual condition – a visualization of man fallen from grace or, as the Protestant Reformer John Calvin (1509–64) put it, man 'corrupted, vitiated, defiled, and destroyed' by sin – a theological diagnosis of humanity's spiritual condition with which Evans readily concurred.[2]

The other formal property that summons allusions to mortality and depravity is the colour of the paintings. With only a few exceptions, all of Evans's pictures are painted uniformly in lamp-black oil.

Interestingly, there are some striking correspondences between the way in which colour and Scripture have been interpreted. The German polymath Wolfgang Goethe (1749–1832), influenced by Origen, conceived of a tripartite interpretation of colour (allegorical, symbolical and mystical), and a threefold purpose for colour (sensual, moral and aesthetic). The 'mystical' corresponds to the spiritual meaning or spiritual application of the colour. The spiritual meaning was conceived not as a specific state of feeling excited by a single colour, but in terms of an analogy. For example, the interrelation of the three primary colours was interpreted (not surprisingly) as a metaphor for the Godhead as Trinity.

In the Western European tradition, the colour black has an established spiritual meaning in part derived from its character in the physical realm (or in the lower storey). For instance, black denotes the absorption of light as opposed to radiance, and so connotatively (in the upper storey) it came to symbolize obscurity and uncleanness. In Old and New Testament culture, black denoted dark-toned things and, allusively, was connected with the negative and evil side of the spiritual realm, suggesting, among other things, a sorrowful spiritual condition, despair, evil, as well as symbolizing the expression and effect of God's judgement on sin. Evans has remarked that he used black because it was the most appropriate colour with which to render the miners. On a physical and denotative level, the colour is one of the dominant characteristics of their working environment. But his use of black is not reserved for the representation of scenes associated with mining alone; it pervades paintings depicting biblical subjects, incidents from Nonconformist history, folk-life and industrial history too. The inordinate darkness either casts these scenes into what seems like perpetual night or places them under an overshadowing, like that which came upon the land of Israel at the Crucifixion (Matthew 27.45). Two thousand years later, that same darkness has spread into the hills, fields, trees and clouds above the pits. In Evans's paintings, the valleys of South Wales become the 'valley of the shadow' (Psalm 23.4).

There are certain compositional affinities between Evans's work and examples of religious art. Several of these modes have been touched upon already. For example, some of the titles of the paintings operate allusively to summon up religious or biblical concepts and scenes; and their colour acts as a vehicle of biblical conflation to unify the world of the Bible and the world of mining (the upper and lower storeys). In his painting *Ecce Homo* (1983), which features a close-up of the face of Christ crucified, Evans engages biblical illustration and, in so doing, shrouds the event with a physical darkness normally associated with his depictions of coalmining. Evans rarely illustrated biblical scenes. Rather, the works summon up biblical or religious concepts indirectly, by way of compositional analogy. *Journey to the Far End* (1979) depicts colliers travelling in drams to their place of work under the charge of the rider who stands on the wire rope outside the last dram. In the bottom right-hand corner of the *Last Judgement* (1535–91), Michelangelo has represented the classical myth of Charon, the official boatman of the Underworld, ferrying the souls of the damned across the River Acheron towards the infernal regions. This myth is evoked pictorially in Evans's picture by the correspondence of the rider at the rear end of the dram with Charon. Likewise, the forlorn cargo of miners compacted into the transport resembles the despairing damned facing their ultimate journey. Metaphorically, both journeys have the same destination (the coal pit was often likened to Hades or hell in the religious culture of the coalminer).

The fusion of mining and religion, of the upper and lower storeys, in these paintings is covert: the (as it were) 'heavenly' sense is evident only when one brings to the works a knowledge of Scripture, religious art and the culture of coalmining in South Wales. However, there is one painting in which the synthesis of the industrial and the biblical is overt, and it is the keystone of Evans's oeuvre: *Entombed – With Jesus in the Midst* (1974) (Figure 11). The image shows a scene underground in a coal mine. Specifically, it depicts the aftermath of a disaster: a section of roof has dropped like a guillotine, shearing two standing posts and imprisoning four miners in the road. Three of the miners are seated. The fourth man kneels and prays fervently in the direction of the last member of the group who, according to the title, is Jesus.

In terms of its denoted aspect the picture (like *'The Trumpet Shall Sound'*) evidently amalgamates mining and religion, secular and religious, the mundane and the profound, reflecting the integration of those themes in the artist's own life and thought. Evans, as has been mentioned, was for much of his life a Pentecostal lay-preacher. Therefore, we should anticipate finding a sermonic or homiletic seam beneath the painting's surface. The homiletic content can be discerned, first, from the connotations summoned by the painting's title. The evocative transitive verb 'entombed' not only describes the miners' current fate but also alludes to Christ's sepulchral burial, from which he rose. This allusion is endorsed by the painting's compositional affinity to Piero della Francesca's (?1420–92) *Resurrection of Christ* (1463–5). Here, Jesus triumphantly mounts the tomb, at the base of which the legionaries (in positions not unlike those of the miners) still slumber. In Piero's scene, Christ holds the long-shafted flag emblematic of his victory over death. Evans substitutes for it the biblical symbol of the lamp, and portrays Christ holding the keys of death and hell. The biblical and theological content of Evans's work is, thus, more extensive, Christ being depicted symbolically both as victor over the grave and as the God of comfort and judgement. Here the lamp, like the one Christ holds in William Holman Hunt's (1827–1910) famous *The Light of the World* (1853–4) (to which *Entombed* bears more than a passing resemblance) symbolizes Christ himself. The title's subheading *With Jesus in the Midst* also has biblical connotations. There are two references in the Gospels to Christ being 'in the midst'. The first is spoken by Christ himself to his disciples in the context of a discourse on prayer: 'For where two or three are gathered together in my name, there am I in the midst of them' (Matthew 18.20). This is the promise of the assured presence of Christ where

Figure 11: Nicholas Evans, *Entombed – With Jesus in the Midst* (1974).
The National Museum, Cardiff.

believers assemble for an act of Christian communion, apprehended spiritually, as an internal and invisible communion of the divine and human spirit. In the painting the experience is objectified: 'Jesus in the midst' becomes a palpable phenomenon. There are several interpretations of this manifestation: first, Christ could be present as a vision (in the Pentecostal and revivalist tradition to which Evans belonged, such appearances were considered a matter of fact); second, the image may represent the visualization of what was merely subjectively experienced, the conferment of apparent form and substance on the unseen spiritual consolation of the miners, so that it may be evident to the spectator. It may also have been intended to convey the conviction that the spiritual presence of Christ was, for the miners, as real as one another's company. In this sense, the work can also be read as a contemporary biblical transposition of another instance of Christ 'in the midst', recorded in the Old Testament story of the fiery furnace into which Nebuchadnezzar cast Shadrach, Meshach and Abednego, and where the son of man miraculously appeared to accompany and preserve the three in their trial (Daniel 3.21–5).

The second reference to Christ 'in the midst' occurs in John's Gospel and its parallel texts, on the day of the Resurrection, when Christ returned to his disciples. The account draws attention to the door of the room being shut, yet unable to bar Christ from access. The scene in the mine represents a similar circumstance. The tons of coal that obstruct the miners' way of escape have not prevented Christ from entering and ministering comfort. The disciple Thomas was invited to place his fingers in the nail prints and thrust his hand into the wound in Christ's side, thus evincing, among other things, that Christ was flesh and blood. (In *Entombed*, a nail print and the wound are clearly visible.) In every other respect, Evans has painted the risen Christ in the same way as he has the miners: Jesus appears fully incarnate, possessing a corporeality con-substantive with that of the others. The difficulty with this interpretation is that, according to the Gospels, Christ is presently not only risen but ascended, a transition that effected a further change to his human nature, which now has the glory of heaven conferred upon it. By abandoning historico-theological realism, Evans represents Christ 'in fashion as a man', thereby stressing the earthly humanity of the God-man, and thus his ability to participate in the sufferings of men and women. Christ's divinity is also signified, by the suggestion of a nimbus or halo about his head, produced by a natural form – the incandescence surrounding the lamp on his cap. The adoption of a naturalized symbolism to designate a halo (in contrast to the artifice of a golden disc or luminous circle used in Roman Catholic art) has a precedent in Holman Hunt's *The Shadow of Death* (1869–73), where a nimbus is intimated by the placing of the arch of a window behind Christ's head.

The naturalization of Christ specifically as a miner also derives from the sermonic tradition of Welsh preaching. The Baptist preacher Christmas Evans (1766–1838) developed a complex mining allegory in a discourse on Zechariah chapter 3, where he describes the Son of God going down to the bottom of a pit (of corruption), in a basket (of the gospel), by the rope (of the Father's commission), to suck unto himself the inflammable methane gas (of sin).[3] In the nineteenth century, the attraction of the imagery of the pit for preachers in South Wales was not only because it was the dominant and unifying motif of the community, grounded in its corporate consciousness. The pit also evoked its counterpart in the Old Testament, with which it both shared the same name and had a close formal correspondence. This was particularly true during the early years of mining when the pit was basically a deep hole in the earth, which is what the term denotes in the Old Testament. The disparity between the two types of pits lay in their respective functions. The biblical concept included holes dug in the ground where prisoners were incarcerated and dead bodies cast. The associations of the pit in its literal sense were therefore captivity, punishment, death and putrefaction. Like Christmas Evans, preachers used the concept of the pit as a metaphor, synonymous in the Bible with physical death, putrefaction and the soul's infection by evil. The pit was, thus, a representation of the coalminers' and (in turn) humankind's spiritual condition outside of Christ. What is more, preachers likened Christ (in his role as redeemer) to the pit rescuer – the man who descended the coal mine to save miners (who were emblematic of sinners) entrapped after explosions or falls. Christmas Evans uses the realities of mining as the basis of this 'double aspect' – a principle derived from Christ's use of parables in which nature and everyday life are regarded as a symbolic system whose literal meaning may have a spiritual application. *Entombed* also highlights the ways in which an image can be not just ambivalent but multivalent – reaching out in several directions at once, in this case to a biblical tradition, a sermonic tradition, a visual tradition and a cultural tradition. These traditions are amalgamated and interact within the picture: the Bible cross-referencing itself, intertextually, explicating the picture (and vice versa); the picture echoing and calling to other religious pictures, creating chains of associations and resonances which are passed through a particular interpretative outlook, belonging to a specific culture, during a certain period in its history.

Art and worship: the Pentecostal mindset

The connection of the upper and lower storeys is manifest in respect to not only mining and religion but also Evans's artistic experience and Pentecostal theology, in particular his experience of creativity and image-making, his view of artistic inspiration, his sense of his own facility and his convictions about his art's purpose and mission. These things were influenced by his Pentecostal mindset – specifically the movement's theology of worship, inspiration, preaching and tongues-speaking. For Evans, art had a spiritual essence and utility; he spiritualized the act of painting by conferring on it the status of a private liturgy: it was for him a means of communion with God, and a hymn of praise and adoration. His sense of the divine was also experienced in the very act of making the picture. He believed that he was aided in the act by a power outside himself. This conviction (he believed) was justified by his lack of any formal training in art. His ability had not (according to him) been the product of human tuition or the acquisition of skills. Painting for Evans was not a hard-won discipline but a gift that had been bestowed upon him – not as a capacity to be honed over a period of time by arduous labour, but fully developed. He described the act of making images in terms of an almost visionary encounter and revelation: 'I look at a board, four feet by four feet, and as I look at the board, I can see the figures on the board; I can see my pictures complete.'[4]

On occasions, Evans referred to his experience of visualization as unsummoned, somewhat surprising: the images were spontaneous, coming upon him all at once. It is, he remarked, like cheating, as though he were painting by numbers. The analogy suggests that he felt as though he had been supplied with a preordained pattern that had only to be followed for the image to be realized. What Evans suggested he 'saw' was a picture projected onto the white ground of the support, perceived with an inner eye. It was a visionary blueprint foretelling and directing the outcome of his labour. The experience has several analogies in Pentecostal culture. Pentecostal ministers, particularly in the early years of the movement, would enter the pulpit without a prepared sermon, believing that they would be led by a direct and spontaneous 'word from the Lord' given to them as they spoke. Evans adopted this idea of the inspired preacher when he described the divine enabling he experienced in painting.

As a preacher himself, Evans believed that he spoke as he was 'led', entirely dependent on the Holy Spirit to fill him with words. Preparatory notes, drafts or a verbatim manuscript were therefore both unnecessary and a hindrance to the delivery of a sermon. Evans claimed that God painted through him in the same way. His paintings were executed spontaneously and directly onto the hardboard support without the intervention of compositional studies or preparatory drawings. Inspiration therefore came, in painting as in preaching, during the performance rather than in the premeditation of the act.

This view of artistic inspiration also has its roots in cultic traditions of the Bible, specifically in the Pentecostal understanding of the New Testament manifestation of the baptism of the Spirit and the gift of speaking in tongues (or glossolalia). Speaking in tongues is understood to be the faculty to speak foreign and unknown or heavenly languages fluently without having undergone the drudgery of learning them, which gift was manifested among the disciples on the day of Pentecost. Analogies can be drawn between some of the formal characteristics and procedures of Evans's paintings and glossolalia. Typically, tongues-speaking involves the repetition of the same basic sounds – a perceived reiteration of patterns of intonations, stresses and the same sounds or group of sounds, like a recurring phrase. In Evans's work there is a corresponding economy of elements and formal patterns that are repeated throughout the body of his work. Chief among these are their format (in all but a few cases four feet square), colour (almost invariably black and white) and subject matter (usually scenes of coalmining). Within the common format (a square) there is a recurrence of a limited range of often simple compositional devices undergirding the arrangement of the painting, in these cases intersecting diagonal and parallel divisions of the square. The figures and objects in foreground, middle distance and background are arranged parallel to the picture surface and hence to one another. He did not deploy single or multi-point perspective in his paintings (a technique that takes time to master and execute). Rather, the compositions are made up of elements – faces or figures – repeated in horizontal or diagonal rows parallel to one another, crowding the surface of the painting. Compositional complexity and decision-making had been reduced by crowding the picture-plane with a single repeated element (usually faces) slung together in parallel rows from the top left to the bottom right of the painting. The cumulative effect of the repetition of a limited range of forms, following a fixed formula of representation, and the avoidance of certain technical difficulties, would contribute to Evans's sense of his ability coming easily to him, a phenomenon which he, like the tongues-speaker, attributed to divine enabling.

The manner in which Evans applied the paint, using only fingers and rags, is also restricted, and the lexicon of mark-making, the vocabulary of gesture, line and pattern he uses to denote objects, remains essentially static. The language of representation is thus generally constant or reiterative. Moreover, the variety of represented objects is limited, due largely to the narrowly defined subject matter. With so many constants, the considerations and decisions Evans had to make in the creation of each painting were arguably far fewer than those encountered by many other artists. This would have facilitated speed of execution and goes some way to explaining his prodigious output, just as the repetition of phrases and the phonemic economy of tongues facilitate fluency of speech.

Evans's gift of painting and the Pentecostal gift of tongues are also analogous in their improvisatory nature. He began his paintings by 'doodling', a procedure of manipulating black paint over a white ground and matching the accidental black marks on the surface of the board with salient features of the miners that congregate his imagination. In the same way novices are sometimes initiated into tongues-speaking by being told to play with a phrase or word, repeating it over and over, gradually increasing the speed of utterance until the sounds trip over themselves to become a jumble, as it were, of either abstract or Hebraic-sounding syllables. Out of this improvisation, as in Evans's doodles with paint, come forms that suggest meaning. These forms constitute, in the case of tongues-speaking, an apparent language: that is, sounds like those of a real language, which appear to have syntax, recurring phrases and a lexicon (though their meaning may be entirely foreign to the speaker). In the case of Evans's painting, these forms resemble objects, people and places.

The subject matter of Evans's painting is, in all but a few cases, not overtly religious. Nevertheless, he was able to use painting as a means of religious worship because of the spirit in which he executed his paintings and the sense of worship he experienced during his making of them, as with tongues-speaking, due to the assumed operation of the Holy Spirit in the creation of the work. Through his painting Evans believed he contacted divinity: he was convinced that God 'spoke' through the medium of pigment and gesture. It was in the realization of being a channel of this divine activity that he experienced the sense of reverence. Like the Spirit that motivates the works, the religious aspect of Evans's paintings is (in some cases) invisible, and typological also. Evans's paintings interpret coalmining in the four senses of medieval exegesis. First, they describe the working conditions and socio-culture of the collier in its literal sense in scenes that illustrate mining history. Second, in a painting such as *Entombed*, we see an aspect of mining illuminated in an allegorical and Christological sense. Third, in as much as Evans draws attention to the miners' (and thus our own) mortality, some of the paintings have a profoundly moral sense. And, fourth, in as much as a painting like *'The Trumpet Shall Sound' – Resurrection* signifies a future hope, his work has an analogical or eschatological dimension too.

In Evans's paintings, the invisible and unseen world exists alongside the visible and seen world. They are a Jacob's ladder between the two storeys of earth and heaven, uniting spirit and matter, mining and religion, biblical and contemporary worlds, and provide an apt metaphor for the thorough and unselfconscious integration of Evans's Christian faith with the rest of his life. This 'double aspect' becomes apparent when Scripture, the iconographic traditions of Western religious painting, the homiletic tradition of Welsh Nonconformity and the pneumanistic theology of Pentecostalism are brought to bear on them. For Evans, each painting was in essence a supernatural picture – an image touched by and bearing the imprint of God – and, like the Incarnation he worshipped, an image in which humanity and divinity are conjoined. As in the painting of the title (evidently), so in many of the other paintings (covertly), Jesus is in the midst of the miners, transfiguring suffering and suffusing light over those who 'sit in darkness and in the shadow of death' (Luke 1.79).

Notes

1   E. H. Gombrich, 'Image and Word in Twentieth-Century Art', *Word and Image*, 1, no. 3 (July–September 1985), 213–41 (p. 221).
2   John Calvin, *Commentary upon the Epistle of Saint Paul to the Romans*, ed. Henry Beveridge (Edinburgh, Calvin Translation Society, 1844), pp. 134–5.
3   Christmas Evans, *Sermons, on Various Subjects*, trans. J. Davies (Beaver: William Henry, 1837), p. 150.
4   Nicholas Evans, [a talk on his life and work], Aberystwyth Arts Centre, 1 July 1983.

Suggested reading

Philip Ariès, *Images of Man and Death*, trans. Helen Weaver (Cambridge, MA.: Harvard University Press, 1985).

Roland Barthes, *Mythologies*, trans. Annette Lavers (London: Vintage, 1993).

John Harvey, *Image of the Invisible: The Visualization of Religion in the Welsh Nonconformist Tradition* (Cardiff: University of Wales Press, 1999).

Plate 1: Giovanni Castiglione, *Rebekah Led by the Servant of Abraham* (1650).
The Barber Institute of Fine Arts, The University of Birmingham.

Plate 2: Matthias Stom, *Isaac Blessing Jacob* (c. 1633–40).
The Barber Institute of Fine Arts, The University of Birmingham.

Plate 3: *The Nativity*. The Bodleian Library, University of Oxford, MS Selden Supra 38, fol. lv.

Plate 4: *The Magi Riding Dromedaries*. The Bodleian Library, University of Oxford, MS Bodl. 764, fol. 45v.

Plate 5: Masaccio, *Peter Healing with his Shadow* (1425).
Brancacci Chapel, Santa Maria del Carmine, Florence.

Plate 6: Michelangelo, *Sistine Ceiling* (1508–12), Sistine Chapel, Rome.

Plate 8: *Christ Pantokrator as the Wisdom of God.* Contemporary icon. Private collection.

Plate 7: *The Anastasis* or *The Descent into Hades.* Contemporary icon. Private collection.

Plate 9: Nicholas Evans, *'The Trumpet Shall Sound' – Resurrection*
(1979). Private collection.

Plate 10: Nicholas Evans, *The Last Bond* (1977).
The National Library of Wales, Aberystwyth.

Plate 11: Lovis Corinth, *Ecce Homo* (1925).
Kunstmuseum Basel.

Plate 12: *Vision of St Bernadette.*
Church of the Holy Name, Fishguard.
Photograph: Martin Crampin.

Plate 13: *The Incarnation.*
From the altar frontal at Bistre, in North Wales.
Photograph: Martin Crampin.

8

The Bible and modern art

PETER FRENCH

In the twentieth century, art depicting biblical scenes was no longer destined solely for ecclesiastical use but rather was seen as a legitimate and powerful means by which to explore the grand narratives of humanity's search for meaning and the transcendent. Biblical characters, events and themes were seen as entirely conversant with the challenges that accompanied twentieth-century progress, especially with regard to the value and place of the human person within creation. Peter French explores the place of the Bible in modern art.

Introduction

Beginning with Post-Impressionism in late nineteenth-century France, and ending with American installation art work of 2004, this chapter seeks to introduce the reader to twentieth-century art that depicts or is influenced by biblical narrative. This introduction unfolds chronologically, examining such historical influences as the two World Wars, artistic movements such as Abstract Expressionism, and artists ranging from Otto Dix to Damien Hirst. It is not intended as a comprehensive synopsis of twentieth-century art (or its artists) but rather highlights art that has been influenced by the biblical text during this tumultuous era. Such influence is quite explicit in Beckmann's *The*

Descent from the Cross but it is not so immediately recognizable in the work of Mark Rothko and appears transformed into pharmaceutical products in a work by Damien Hirst. Such diverse forms of art have all been influenced strongly by the Bible in many original and creative ways. This chapter explores that important influence and its impact on some of the twentieth century's major artists.

Post-Impressionism, the First World War and German Expressionism

Two items often found in doctors' and dentists' waiting rooms include dog-eared copies of last year's popular magazines and poster reproductions of Impressionist and Post-Impressionist paintings. Be it Monet's *Water Lilies* or Van Gogh's *Starry Night*, these beautiful images have become commonplace in such public spaces. Given the reassuring nature of their imagery, it is not surprising that we find them in such locations where one could be awaiting a dire diagnosis or the dentist's drill. This is no coincidence. This period of European painting at the end of the nineteenth century accompanied one of the most peaceful periods of modern European history, and, in turn, has produced such popular and iconic images of colour, peace and tranquillity. During this period, many of Europe's most accomplished painters, such as Monet and Cézanne, turned their attention inward towards domestic scenes of rest and relaxation, and outward only to idyllic landscapes. Monet's lilies and garden scenes were painted within the domestic confines of the artist's own private garden, images that delight the eye but also make no reference to the 'outside' world of politics, current events or international affairs.

It is, then, not surprising that in 1889 the French painter Paul Gauguin painted a rather placid depiction of the crucifixion of Jesus. *Le Christ jaune* (the yellow Christ) locates the Crucifixion of Jesus in a rural French setting, much as Italian and Dutch painters before him had painted the events of the life of Jesus within their own familiar geography. Jesus is crucified (Matthew 27.35; Mark 15.25; Luke 23.33; John 19.23) against a backdrop of predominantly yellow meadows, with rolling hills, a nearby village, soft orange trees and a stone wall. Three women in traditional Breton attire sit at the foot of the cross, in prayer or at rest. In the distance a man can be seen climbing over the stone wall to the field beyond. It is a rural, idyllic scene. Jesus is crucified at the forefront of the painting, his crossed and nailed feet resting on a plinth, his arms outstretched with hands nailed to the extremities of the cross bar. The top of the cross – usually the location for Pilate's INRI sign (John 19.19) – is unseen, removed by the top limit of the canvas. Christ is indeed yellow, but a yellow that is completely conversant with the colour themes of the painting.

Such an image of the crucified Christ is analogous with this period of painting born from European peace and at the end of a century in which painters had continued to paint 'traditional' depictions of the crucified Christ. With Impressionism and Post-Impressionism, a shift was occurring in art history, where the emphasis was no longer based upon the reality of an image, but rather on its idealized form. In *Le Christ jaune*, Gauguin was not strictly adhering to the Gospel accounts of Jesus's Crucifixion but rather favouring his own personal desire to locate such a scene within his fascination with Brittany. The strangeness of a 'yellow' Jesus, in both paint and title, was a sign of things to come, where traditional depictions of Christ's Crucifixion would give way to a century of images of a barely recognizable Jesus, set in backgrounds equally unusual or irrelevant to the biblical text. Gauguin's fascination with the countryside of Brittany, its people, rites and culture, and his own desire for faith are the inspiration for *Le Christ jaune*, rather than any proposed function as a focus or location of Christian worship.

We can observe in the twentieth century the removal of the connection between the depiction of a biblical text and a distinctive doctrinal or ecclesiastical purpose. The intention of such art is independent – it is art in and of itself, rather than as an aid to devotion or doctrine, or being simply decoration. No longer under the auspices or patronage of the Church, many twentieth-century art-works influenced by the biblical narrative were created for non-ecclesiastical settings. Such art removed from ecclesiastical intention is a relatively new phenomenon. The painting or sculpture may be intended for private purchase and its new home a domestic setting rather than a chapel or church. In this way, the artist of the twentieth century is also increasingly uninhibited to produce work that affirms or rejects 'traditional' understandings of Christianity. This is a critical juncture in the history of so-called 'Christian' art. Eleven years after Gauguin's death, the peace underpinning Impressionism was shattered by the outbreak of war. As the First World War changed the face of history, so too it was to radically alter the manner in which artists depicted the world. This is especially true of artists interested in depicting biblical scenes and figures.

The German Max Beckmann is no exception. In 1917 Beckmann painted one of the twentieth century's first truly shocking images of Christ. *The Descent from the Cross* is his painting of the dead Christ being removed from the cross in a manner that reminds the viewer that *rigor mortis* has set in. Christ is stiff and wooden, his face permanently affixed in the pain of his death. The ladder used to remove the corpse from the cross forms the centrepiece of the painting, rather than the cross itself. The body of Jesus fills the canvas diagonally, his feet at the bottom left of the canvas, his head top right, his stiff outstretched arms at the opposite corners. Beckmann painted Jesus with white, grey and yellow paints, a body emaciated and skeletal, pale and wan, and with the wounds of his death plain to see. Gone is the comfortable scene of peaceful countryside and quiet attendant villagers; rather, this scene is painted against the backdrop of a dry, dusty earth; a red angry sun hangs in the sky, and the attendant figures are neither perfectly dressed nor peaceful. A snarling man wrangles Christ from the cross while his elder packs up the ladder used to remove the body.

The sinister dirt and ladders of trench warfare are hinted at here; this is a Christ dying at the hands of the malevolent, just as so many of Beckmann's countrymen were dying at the hands of war. Gauguin's ordered fields and peaceful attendants have given way to ruptured earth and scorched bodies.

Beckmann was not alone in setting the biblical text amid the horrors of trench warfare. He was a member of the painterly movement now referred to as German Expressionism; fellow artists in this period included Otto Dix, George Grosz, Max Ernst and Lovis Corinth, in whose art we can see their reaction to the excesses of the warfare they observed around them. Dix in particular was at the forefront of producing images of wounded soldiers and trench warfare, while also depicting what he perceived as modern industrialists becoming fat and wealthy from war profits. Many of his paintings reference the Bible, especially those later in his career. For example, his *Matthaus Evangelium* (The Gospel of Matthew) is a set of lithographs containing many events from that particular Gospel. Dix, who became infamous for his gory depictions of war wounds, is no less brutal in his illustration of scenes from this Gospel. His *Flight into Egypt* illustrates the Holy Family's escape to Egypt to avoid Herod's slaughter of all the infants in Bethlehem (Matthew 2.13–18). Dix draws the escape with heavy, fast and almost childlike strokes, his black pencil drawing a German soldier wresting a screaming baby from the arms of its wide-eyed and horrified mother. Such identification of the timeless elements of the Gospel stories and their relevance for events of the twentieth century is important to note. As we shall discover, with the twentieth century's radical progress and change, the manner in which artists chose to imagine the Bible is also radically transformed.

In 1918, the last year of the war, the English sculptor Eric Gill installed 14 *Stations of the Cross*, commissioned for the nave of Westminster Cathedral, London. A gifted sculptor, Gill's exquisitely carved stone images of Christ's journey from condemnation to burial are very different from the rawness of German Expressionism. The *Stations* were Gill's first major commission, and his restrained, timeless imagery was influenced by the Art Deco movement, the scenes of each Station like Babylonian temple reliefs. The soldiers who give Christ his cross in Station Two (*Jesus Receives his Cross*) are passive figures, appearing passionless about the torture they are inflicting. There are no angry soldiers or scenes from the trenches, rather a depiction of the timeless elements of human suffering, of soldiers under authority, of a victim condemned to die. Each Station is unadorned stone, save for the painted gold haloes of the holy persons and the red wounds of Christ's hands and feet. Gill's attention to the biblical narrative is highlighted by the inclusion of the biblical text in some of the Stations, written in Latin.

These Stations were not without controversy, however. The stylized nature of the imagery, their simplicity and their 'foreign nature' caused much concern, as did the moral character of the sculptor himself. A man of great religiosity and Christian faith, Gill was nevertheless a controversial figure for such a commission. Regardless, the Cathedral supported their installation and in 1940 further commissioned Gill to sculpt the altarpiece for the Chapel of St George and the English Martyrs. Gill would die only one month after its completion.

The German painter Lovis Corinth was no stranger to personal suffering. A manic-depressive whose search for a salve for his troubled soul led him to alcoholism, Corinth suffered a stroke in 1911, deepening his personal experience of pain and physical limitation. His timeless painting *Ecce Homo* ('Here is the man', John 19.5, see Plate 11) shows Jesus immediately after his flagellation at the behest of Pontius Pilate. Hands manacled, the crown of thorns upon his head, Christ's brow is furrowed with the strain of physical exhaustion. Corinth paints Jesus as a man like himself, constrained and restricted by the limits of his physical being, his personal association with the painting further emphasized by the figure of Pontius Pilate, whose hand on Christ's shoulder points to Corinth's signature. Christ the liberator has become the prisoner; Christ the healer has become the wounded.

Jesus is painted with a politician on one side, a soldier on the other, caught literally between political authority and military might, which is exactly what John chapter 19 describes. Christ's downcast demeanour is in contrast to the expressions of his captors: Pontius Pilate strangely benign and the professional soldier smug and superior. This soldier is painted in a uniform not dissimilar to those that Corinth would have observed marching through his home city of Berlin. Corinth depicts Jesus in his robe, a streak of red on a washed-out canvas, the figure bringing life and colour to an otherwise grey and bleak scene. Jesus appears to plead with the viewer to be released, holding out his hands in supplication. His face and arms are flecked with the blood of his flagellation, a foretaste of the blood that will flow when he is nailed to the cross. The wide brush-strokes and indistinct nature of the background remove the painting from a specific time or context, suggesting that this is a timeless image. Lovis Corinth was a prolific artist, accomplished in drawing and etching as well as in painting, producing nearly 1,000 works in his life. During the Third Reich (1933–45), paintings and etchings that Corinth had completed after his stroke in 1911 were deemed as 'degenerate' by the State and removed from general public display. Hitler's Germany recognized Corinth's criticism of its political and military figures that, like Pilate, subjected the innocent to the extremes of intolerance and injustice.

A year after Corinth's death in 1926, his contemporary Max Ernst created controversy and drew public attention with his painting entitled *The Blessed Virgin Chastises the Infant Jesus before Three Witnesses: A.B., P.E. and the Artist* (Figure 12). Painted in oil on canvas, this two-metre square painting shows a strident Mary spanking the infant Jesus. While the Gospels do not record such an event as taking place, the question of how Mary disciplined the infant Christ is nevertheless an intriguing one. Viewers of this painting were shocked to see the Messiah, God's chosen, bent over the knee of his mother, receiving a hiding for what one can only assume was bad behaviour. Countless images of the infant Jesus in Renaissance art had inured people against the surprise of seeing Jesus naked, but apparently such imagery did not prepare them for Jesus's rosy bottom, red from spanking. Furthermore, Ernst paints the Christ-child's halo as having fallen from above his head and lying on the ground at his mother's feet. Peering through a window, the three witnesses to this scene, who at first glance appear as the Magi, are in fact the artist and his artistic colleagues André Breton and Paul Eluard.

Such an image of Christ was deemed blasphemous, and the Archbishop of Cologne closed the exhibition in which it was displayed. Ernst's own father also denounced the painting. Whether one thinks the image blasphemous or not, the nature of the painting raises intriguing theological questions that simply are not suggested by more demure reproductions of the Holy Family's domestic arrangements. As we understand Christ as sinless, does this mean he never misbehaved as a child, and never drew the wrath of his parents? What right does Mary, the God-bearer, have to strike the Son of God? While we learn from the New Testament that Jesus has all authority placed at his feet (Matthew 28.18), what authority does the much adored Virgin Mary have?

Ernst's subversion of a traditionally serene image of Mary and Jesus was in line with his leadership of the Dada group in Cologne. Dada was founded by sculptor Hans Jean Arp in Zurich in 1916 and was an organization of artists and radicals who sought to destroy all traditional forms of art by appealing to the ridiculous and absurd. Their name 'Dada' was a senseless word picked randomly from the dictionary; in French *dada* means 'hobbyhorse'. The Dadaists, with Ernst and Dix among them, plead for a return to an almost childlike society in which spontaneous joy, ridiculous costumes and new music were a response to the bloodletting and moral bankruptcy they perceived in the First World War.

Stanley Spencer's *The Resurrection of the Soldiers* (1928–9) offered

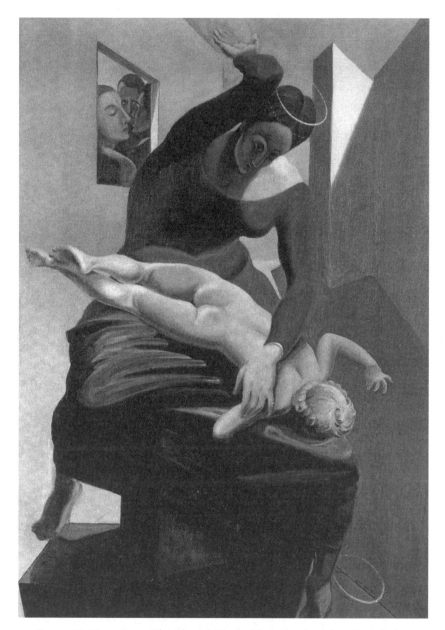

Figure 12: Max Ernst, *The Blessed Virgin Chastises the Infant Jesus before Three Witnesses: A.B., P.E. and the Artist* (1926). Museum Ludwig, Cologne.
Photocredit: Rheinisches Bildarchiv Cologne.

yet another kind of subversion. Painted for the east wall of the Sandham Memorial Chapel in Hampshire, England, Spencer's enormous image of the Resurrection does not place Christ as the centre of the piece, but rather a great pile of tumbling white crosses. These crosses, so familiar at war cemeteries, have been uprooted and cast aside as the soldiers buried beneath them rise in the Resurrection. Restored to life, soldiers walk about the graveyard, and a horse upsets its rider and cart at this unsettling scene. This is similar to Matthew's version of what happens at the time of Jesus's death, where in Matthew 27.53 the tombs 'were opened and many bodies of the saints who had fallen asleep were raised'. Spencer's imagination fired this painting, where those slaughtered in the war are given new life in an almost dream-like depiction of the fulfilment of Jesus's promise.

Surrealism and abstraction

Dreams were the subject of much admiration by a group of painters known as the Surrealists. Pioneered by André Breton in France in the 1920s, Surrealist artists include Paul Klee, Alberto Giacometti and Salvador Dalí. Such artists were interested in the human subconscious, its images unsullied by interpretation, and in the raw, uncompromised, pure images of Freud's dream world. This search for purity found much inspiration in the understanding and depiction of dreams, those unfettered images constantly drawn on the canvas of the brain. This search for purity saw no problem extending its reach beyond what was reasonable and sane to what was subversive or mad. Many painters before them had painted the mad, notably Hieronymus Bosch (c. 1450–1516), but few had chosen to depict the hallucinatory images of the mad. The attraction of such images was that they were the total opposite of reason, wisdom and sanity. At first glance, such a preoccupation might preclude these artists from painting scenes from the Bible. This was not the case, however, and we can observe depictions

of biblical texts and stories in the oeuvre of perhaps the Surrealists'
most famous exponent, Salvador Dalí.

The eccentric and self-centred Dalí was born a Catholic but, like
many of his fellow Surrealists, was a staunch atheist. This did not
prevent him from being attracted to the biblical narrative. Dalí painted
many biblical scenes, including depictions of Mary holding the infant
Jesus and Jesus's Crucifixion and Ascension. Perhaps his most famous
Christian painting, *Christ of Saint John of the Cross*, introduced a new
way of seeing the Crucifixion of Jesus. We look down at Christ's body
as if we are perched on the top of the cross itself. The cross is suspended
above the earth, pointing down at the Bay of Port Lligat, Spain, and its
unusual perspective reflects Dalí's general desire to change the way in
which the viewer interacts with images. Suspended in the sky, Dalí
locates the Crucifixion both in and out of geography, on earth and also
in heaven.

Dalí's contemporary René Magritte was also intrigued by the subversion of reality. In *La Trahison des images (Ceci n'est pas une pipe)*
Magritte paints a pipe used for smoking. Underneath is written, '*Ceci
n'est pas une pipe*' ('This is not a pipe'). Initially, this would appear to
be a contradiction: the painting is obviously of a pipe, yet the words
underneath tell us that it is not a pipe. The point that Magritte makes
here is that while we recognize the image of the pipe as a pipe, it is in
fact not a pipe but rather a painting of a pipe. The painting is real, the
frame is real, the image is real, yet it is truly impossible to say, 'that is a
pipe', only, 'that is an image of a pipe'. While Magritte cannot lay claim
to be an illustrator of the biblical text, Magritte's painting foreshadows
a disconnection between imagery and reality that radically changes the
course of art in the twentieth century. As the century progresses, Surrealist images give way to paintings that no longer depict immediately
recognizable places, people or things. This is a critical juncture to note,
for we witness for the first time a sustained period in art history where
abstract images of the world, and of the Bible, become prevalent.

Abstract images are images that are not immediately identifiable as known objects, figures or scenes. Abstract Expressionist works were often large blocks of single colour on a canvas, random shapes or differing shades of the same colour. With the outbreak of the Second World War in 1939, many artists fled Europe, fearing persecution for their art, and with them the centre of avant-garde art shifted from Europe to America – especially New York. Here artists such as Jackson Pollock, Mark Rothko, Willem de Kooning, Franz Kline, Robert Motherwell and Adolph Gottlieb painted increasingly abstract works, with large canvases often saturated with raw colour. Pollock, often considered the forefather of the movement now termed Abstract Expressionism, painted his canvases on the floor, walking around them, and applying layer upon layer of dripped and splashed paint, creating paintings without the use of a single brush-stroke. The results are very random works, alive with colour, cross-hatched, the layered paint creating a landscape of its own.[1]

The painters Barnett Newman and Mark Rothko are of particular interest. Newman was a native New Yorker born in 1905 to Polish-Jewish immigrant parents. Not content with his painting before 1940, he destroyed all of these works, took four years off and recommenced painting in 1944. Remaining unpopular with the press and the public for much of his ensuing career, it was only after 1960 that he began to achieve his now iconic status in modern art history. A significant turning point in this late career was the painting of a series of works entitled *Stations of the Cross (Lema Sabachthani)* that went on display at the Guggenheim Museum in New York in 1966 (Figure 13). Primarily influenced by Christ's cry of 'Why have you forsaken me?' as recorded in Matthew 27.46 and Mark 15.34, Christ's reiteration of the opening verse of Psalm 22 was, for Newman, a profound phrase that articulated one of the deepest cries of humanity.

Part of Newman's unpopularity was due to the extreme abstraction of his work. This is true of his *Stations* series, a collection of 14 black and white paintings on equally sized unprepared canvases painted over a period of eight years. Newman used a mixture of oil and syn-

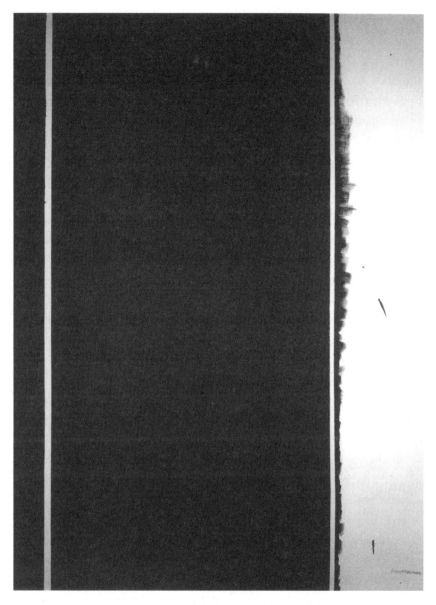

Figure 13: Barnett Newman, *Twelfth Station*, Robert and Jane Meyerhoff
Collection.
Image © 2007 Board of Trustees, National Gallery of Art, Washington, 1965,
acrylic on canvas, 1.981 × 1.524 m (78 × 60 ins).

155

thetic paint to achieve his trademark restricted imagery, painting a small number of vertical lines on a white, black or unprimed part of the canvas. Newman referred to his trademark lines as 'zips', and in the *Stations* series they are a predominant feature. Newman painted these zips with either clean edges or thickly, the black or white paint bleeding into the surrounding area. Each painting in the series is unique, the zips are spaced differently, the juxtaposition of black against white shifting with each canvas. Such movement of key elements in each canvas suggests the manner in which characters in any drama vary their positions and moods, altering the way in which they relate to each other and the viewer. Although greatly influenced by the cry of Jesus on the cross, the *Stations* do not attempt to depict the traditional imagery of the devotional Stations of the Cross, but rather offer spaces in which to meditate upon Jesus's cry of dereliction. The canvases themselves are a 'human scale for the human cry'.[2] The cry of dereliction was for Newman a question that had not, and could not, be answered. His mission instead was to engage the viewer as directly and as simply as possible, evoking personal feelings which in turn gave the painting its meaning:

> Instead of making cathedrals out of Christ, man or 'life', we
> are making it out of ourselves, out of our own feelings. The
> image we produce is the self-evident one of revelation, real
> and concrete, that can be understood by anyone who will look
> at it without the nostalgic glasses of history.[3]

Compared to Newman, the work of Mark Rothko is a step further away from the narrative text, yet his paintings must be considered when discussing modern art that draws us closer to the sublime and to God. Like his predecessor Wassily Kandinsky, who commented that 'colour directly influences the soul',[4] Rothko was fascinated by the idea that the experience of raw and pure colour, at a size far larger than the observer, drew the viewer into the sublime and in this way had transcendent qualities. Rothko's paintings are large, overwhelming canvases that in his later period consist of two or three large blocks of colour creating an undefined, yet no less powerful, sense of transcendence and peace.[5] By his own admission, Rothko was 'interested only in expressing basic human emotions. The people who weep before my pictures are having the same religious experience I had when painting them.'[6]

While Rothko did not illustrate the biblical text *per se*, his was the crucial contribution to the construction and decoration of the Rothko Chapel in Houston, Texas. Alongside the Matisse Chapel in Vence and the Chapel in Ronchamp by Le Corbusier (both in France), the Rothko Chapel remains as one of the twentieth century's most significant intersections of modern art and religion. Containing 14 of his large paintings, the Chapel has become an international site of multi-faith worship, inspired by the transcendent nature of the paintings themselves. The forecourt of the Chapel contains Barnett Newman's sculpture *Broken Obelisk*, dedicated to Dr Martin Luther King, Jr.

Painting at the same time as Newman and Rothko was the Irish-born British artist Francis Bacon. His was a noticeably more violent approach to the spiritual dimension of painting. In his *Three Studies for a Crucifixion*, painted in 1962, Bacon mimicked the triptych style that decorated Christian altars of the Middle Ages and Renaissance. Such altars are the site for the celebration of the Eucharist and thus the remembrance of Christ's life and death. Paintings illustrating these sites were most often placed above the altar itself and divided into three separate boards or canvases. In his own triptych, Bacon's illustration of a crucifixion is not intended for such a sacred location, but rather uses such a reference as a means of highlighting the link his painting has with the overtly Christian paintings usually portrayed in such fashion. Bacon was himself an avowed atheist, but his response to the violence of the Second World War and the degradation humanity suffered provoked such a deep response that he began painting his own versions of Jesus's Crucifixion from the mid 1930s.

Thus this painting of 1962 is a mature statement of his work and a reflection of his enduring commitment to exploring human suffering through the lens of the Crucifixion of Christ.

In *Three Studies for a Crucifixion* Bacon continues to explore the visceral nature of the act of crucifixion itself, rather than any spiritual or salvific dimension. In each canvas a twisted carcass appears, cut open and splayed, with bones, blood and meat clearly visible. In the left canvas two people appear as political or bureaucratic figures, one open-mouthed and in a mocking pose, the other with a haunted look and pointing towards the central panel. This panel, the focus of the work, displays a contorted and bloodied human figure lying on a bed made of white, jutting ribs. Three windows behind the figure have black blinds pulled down to their sills – there is no view of the outside world, no light or hope entering this scene. To the right a butcher's hung animal carcass dominates the panel, with a ghostly humanoid shadow moving towards it on the floor. Bacon's *Crucifixion* is a bloody scene, conversant with the reality of torturing a human body with nails and wood. Viewed with the Passion narratives in mind, the viewer is reminded of the extreme violence endured by Jesus.

Ben Willikens' *Abendmahl* (Last Supper) shares some key features with Bacon's work but illustrates a very different scene from the New Testament (Figure 14). Like Bacon's *Crucifixion*, this painting is also a triptych and those same references to the Eucharist especially apply here. This large painting, measuring 3 × 6 metres, dominates the space in which it is hung at the German Museum of Architecture in Frankfurt-am-Main, and recalls the size of the canvases favoured by the Abstract Expressionists. Essentially the painting is a rewriting – or revisiting – of Leonardo da Vinci's famous *l'Ultima Cena* (The Last Supper) in the refectory of the Convent of Santa Maria delle Grazie in Milan. Willikens's reading of the Last Supper is very different from da Vinci's, primarily for *Abendmahl*'s complete absence of figures or actions. Yet when we view the painting, we cannot help but be reminded of da Vinci's work and the account of the Last Supper in all four Gospels

(Matthew 26.20–29, Mark 14.17–26, Luke 22.14–23, John 13.21–30 and in Paul's first letter to the Corinthians (11.23–26).

Willikens paints the location and setting for Jesus's Last Supper in a strangely clinical setting, the centrepiece of the work a long table with rubber feet resting on a sterile tiled floor. The table is clothed with a pristine white sheet, bearing no marks, stains or blood. To its left and right are closed steel doors similar to those found in a morgue, hospital or prison. We are not privy to where they lead. Most captivating about this painting is the artist's rendering of light. Behind the table are a doorway and two windows leading into a room filled with white light. This light illuminates the entire painting, reflecting on the cold steel of the doors and on the surface of the floor. The viewer is unaware as to what the source of this light is yet it dominates the painting and has a transcendent quality. For those familiar with the biblical texts describing the Last Supper, Willikens's work is an unmistakable interpretation of the event, describing the continuing light, presence and action of God long after Jesus and the disciples left the upper room. In the aftermath of *The Da Vinci Code*, the viewer of

Figure 14: Ben Willikens, *Abendmahl* (Last Supper) (1976–9).
Deutsches Architekturmuseum, Frankfurt am Main.

Abendmahl is refreshingly reminded that it is the power of God in Christ that is revealed at the Last Supper, not the particularities of the guest list . . . !

Sculpture, installation art and art of the late twentieth century

So far we have concentrated upon drawings and paintings of the narrative text. Needless to say there are very many examples of other media depicting biblical stories and themes, including sculpture, installation art and electronic media, that we have not included in this chapter, but their absence by no means diminishes their significance.

One sculptor who has had a profound influence upon twentieth-century art concerned with the biblical text is the American George Segal. In his work *In Memory of May 4, 1970: Kent State – Abraham & Isaac*, Segal explores the precise moment in Genesis 22 where Abraham raises his knife to kill his son Isaac – as a test of Abraham's faithfulness to God. Segal sculpted this piece in response to the killings of 4 May 1970 in which National Guardsmen opened fire on students at Kent State University, Ohio, killing four and wounding nine others. The students were protesting against America's incursion into Cambodia of 25 April 1970, which saw an escalation of the Vietnam War and an expansion of hostilities that many feared would involve further drafting of civilians into the military.

Isaac is depicted on his knees, his hands bound with rope, his face raised towards his father. Abraham leans menacingly over him, a sharp knife in his right hand pointing directly at Isaac's chest, stepping forward with his left foot in the frozen moment before thrusting the knife into his son's heart. As we know from Genesis 22.11, at the very last moment God stays the execution, sending an angel to intervene now that God has tested Abraham's obedience. Segal's sculpture is powerful because the figures are life-size and threatening; one can see first hand the violence of the scene. The observer can easily imagine being one or other person in the drama and can thus imagine all the swirl of emotions that would come with such involvement. Segal believed that the tragedy of the Kent State shootings hinged upon the equal conviction of the students and the guardsmen, just as the equal convictions of both Abraham and Isaac drew them into potential tragedy. Segal explained: 'It's an attempt to introduce difficult moral and ethical questions as to how older people should behave toward their children.'[7]

In an equally thought-provoking fashion as much of his other art-work, the infamous English artist Damien Hirst offered his own version of *The Last Supper* in 1999. *The Last Supper* is a direct reference to the biblical text, yet bears no visual reference to the text or its characters whatsoever. The work consists of 13 individual posters (an obvious reference to the number of people present at the Last Supper) depicting boxes containing clinical drugs such as morphine, saquinavir and lamivudine. The typeface, format and colours are similar to the phar-maceutical product yet Hirst has subverted these labels, replacing a clinical name with a familiar British food staple such as Mushroom, Chicken and Cornish Pasty. Thus one poster reads:

Chicken
Concentrated Oral Solution
Morphine Sulphate
20mg/ml
Each 1ml contains Morphine
Sulphate BP 20mg
120ml.

The artist has replaced the pharmaceutical company's name with 'Damien Hirst' and the ever-present company logo with a stylized phallic symbol. One could dismiss such a work as being simply playful or subversive – which *Last Supper* certainly is – but Hirst is also making a more profound point. The last meal that Jesus shares with his friends institutes the Eucharist as a primary means of remembering him. In such an act of remembrance, communicants take into themselves the so-described body and blood of Christ, ingesting that which is divine. There is much evidence of Christ as healer in the New Testament (see Matthew 4.24–25; Mark 2.1–12; Luke 4.38–44; John 9.1–7) and here Hirst is drawing a connection between medicine and miracles and asking questions about what one places more belief in – faith or science? The drugs mentioned in the work are drugs used in treating HIV/AIDS and terminal stages of human illness, and so the suite of paintings also raises questions about the transformative effect of chemicals and faith in the face of death.

The title of Jim Hodges's 2004 installation piece, *don't be afraid*, is a colloquial abbreviation of the recurring phrase in the New Testament 'do not be afraid' found in the Gospels (Matthew 1.20, 10.31, 14.27, 17.7, 28.5, 10; Mark 6.50; Luke 1.13, 30, 2.10, 5.10, 12.7, 32; John 6.20, 12.15; Acts 18.9, 27.24 and Revelation 1.17). In 2002 Hodges invited over 90 delegates to the United Nations to translate this phrase into their native languages. He then reprinted these phrases on varying sizes of billboards and enormous pieces of material, affixing them to the exteriors of various museums. *don't be afraid* has been exhibited in Worcester, Massachusetts, London, Miami, Chicago, Washington D.C. and Santiago de Compostela, Spain. Hodges believes that the phrase evokes 'a sense of peace and freedom from fear'[8] that is worth hearing across national, cultural and language barriers. While it is difficult to determine the extent to which Hodges is directly referring to the biblical text, Christians across the world will readily identify this statement as a key message of Jesus's ministry and a phrase firmly rooted in the Bible. The artist's intention is to use his art as a counter to the culture of fear propagated by the terrorism of these first years of the twenty-first century.

Conclusion

The savagery and bloodshed of the First World War saw the way in which Jesus of the New Testament was imagined and depicted. The experience of extreme violence and massive loss of life prompted artists to depict Jesus as one of those who also suffered at the hands of the malevolent, changing for ever the way in which twentieth-century audiences would view the Christ. Gone were placid rural scenes of an 'idyllic' Crucifixion, replaced instead by images of Jesus as a scourged pleading prisoner or as dead, stiff and mangled just like the corpses of trench warfare. With the violent excesses of the first half of the twentieth century, artists were able to identify the grand themes of the biblical narrative with the profound questions large-scale war and technological development were asking of humanity.

Art depicting scenes from the Bible was no longer destined solely for ecclesiastical use but rather was seen as a legitimate and powerful means by which to explore the grand narratives of humanity's search for meaning and the transcendent in the twentieth century. Biblical characters, events and themes were seen as entirely conversant with the challenges that accompanied twentieth-century progress, especially with regard to the value and place of the human person within creation. After the Holocaust, how could humanity understand itself to be loved by God and charged with the commission to love one's neighbour as oneself? Artists such as Francis Bacon and Barnett Newman responded to such questions in very different ways, both challenging the viewer's understanding of the relationship between the Bible's testimony of humanity's experience of God and the twentieth century's own explorations of such a relationship.

The biblical text with its rich record of humanity's experience of God has always been a source of inspiration and stimulation for artists and art viewers alike. In the twentieth century this enchantment with the biblical narrative continued in a most exciting and provocative fashion, challenging us to rethink long-held beliefs about 'what is art' and inviting us again to view our world through the lens of the biblical narrative.

Notes

1 For a fine example of such work, see Jackson Pollock, *Blue Poles: Number 11, 1952* (1952).
2 As quoted in <www.barnettnewman.org/chronology.php>, '1966'.
3 M. Baigell, 'Barnett Newman's Stripe Paintings and Kabbalah: A Jewish Take', in *American Art* (Chicago: University of Chicago Press, 1994), p. 36.
4 See F. Birren, *History of Colour in Painting* (New York: Reinhold, 1965).
5 See, for example, Mark Rothko, *No.14, 1960* (1960).
6 Mark Rothko as quoted in *Celebrating the 40th Anniversary of the Rothko Chapel Commission, April 18–19, 2004* (Houston: The Rothko Chapel, 2004), p. 5.
7 See <http://speccoll.library.kent.edu/4may70/exhibit/memorials/segal.html>.
8 Installation guide for *Directions – Jim Hodges, don't be afraid, 2005–2006* (Washington D.C.: Smithsonian, Hirshhorn Museum and Sculpture Garden), p. 2.

Suggested reading

R. Crumlin, *Beyond Belief: Modern Art and the Religious Imagination* (Melbourne, Australia: National Gallery of Victoria, 1998).

J. Elderfield (ed.), *Modern Painting and Sculpture: 1880 to the Present at the Museum of Modern Art* (New York: The Museum of Modern Art, 2004).

E. G. Heller (ed.), *Reluctant Partners: Art and Religion in Dialogue* (New York: The Gallery at the American Bible Society, 2004).

9

Biblical images of Mary in the visual tradition of Wales

SARAH BOSS

The biblical figure of Mary is central to Christian iconography. In this chapter, Sarah Boss focuses on those aspects of the rich iconographic traditions that provide the viewer with insights into the role given to Mary by the Gospel writers and in church tradition. She takes her examples from specific locations in Wales, home to many distinctive images of the Virgin.

Introduction

This chapter considers nineteenth- and twentieth-century images of the Virgin Mary distinctive to the visual tradition of Wales, found principally in church settings, either Roman Catholic or the Church in Wales (Anglican). In harmony with the general theme of the book, most of the images are inspired by the Bible; while some are principally for decoration or embellishment, others are objects for devotion, and in several instances there is no clear boundary between the two. My own interest is primarily in the theological meanings implicit in biblical visual imagery relating to the Virgin and the examples I use by way of illustration are taken from the rich and distinctive iconography of Mary found in Wales. The chapter is intended as an introduction to this area of Marian study, and for ease of access I have organized the sections to accord with the chronology of Mary's life.

The conception of the Virgin

Let us start with images that are concerned with the very beginning of Mary's life: her conception. The doctrine of the Immaculate Conception maintains that the Virgin Mary was conceived by her parents – traditionally known as St Anne and St Joachim – without the stain of original sin. Thus, unlike the conception of Jesus, Mary's conception was not virginal, but occurred through sexual intercourse. According to Western church teaching, one of the consequences of Adam and Eve's fall from grace is that all humanity is now conceived in a state of sin, called 'original sin'. This sin is washed away at Baptism. However, the teaching of the Roman Catholic Church holds that the Virgin Mary, by a special grace of God, was preserved from original sin, so that her conception was 'immaculate', i.e. 'stainless'. The story of Mary's conception, birth and childhood probably dates back at least as far as the second century, but the ancient texts say nothing about original sin or Mary's exemption from it. It was from the eleventh century onwards that the doctrine of Mary's Immaculate Conception was discussed and disputed, and it was officially defined as an article of Catholic faith in 1854.

In the sixteenth century, the promoters of the doctrine of the Immaculate Conception wanted a clear visual image by which the doctrine could be represented. Such an image would be used to inspire devotion, and also form part of the campaign for the doctrine's acceptance as an official part of Catholic teaching. The image that was finally successful in this effort was formulated by artists in Seville, most especially Francisco Pacheco (1564–1644). In his textbook *The Art of Painting*, inspired by the visions of a Portuguese holy woman, Beatriz de Silva, Pacheco combined and consolidated earlier iconographic types to produce one of the most popular forms of representation that the Western world has ever seen. Its purest manifestation is, perhaps, *The Virgin of the Immaculate Conception* painted by Pacheco's son-in-law, Diego Velásquez (Figure 15).

Figure 15: Diego Velásquez, *The Virgin of the Immaculate Conception*.
The National Gallery, London. Bought with the aid of The Art Fund, 1974.

Velásquez's painting alludes to three passages of Scripture. The first of these is the Song of Songs; the second is Proverbs 8.22–31; and the third is Apocalypse (or Revelation) 12. We shall not consider here the reference to the Song of Songs, since explicit references to this book are lost from later Marian images of the kind that are so well represented in Wales. Proverbs 8, however, continues to have echoes in the later iconography. The passage in question begins with the words, 'The Lord created me at the beginning of his ways, the first of his acts of old.' These words are spoken by the figure of Wisdom, who goes on to say that she was present with God from before the creation of the earth, and, indeed, before God divided the waters at the foundation of the cosmos. From the eighth century, this text was used as a reading for liturgies on the feasts of Mary's nativity and conception. The words were applied to Mary, and were seen as suitable since they indicated that Mary had been chosen and prepared by God from all eternity to be the mother of God incarnate. In the fourteenth century, those who supported the doctrine of the Immaculate Conception argued that, since Mary had been prepared for her great office and task from before the foundation of the world, she would not have been subject to the sin of Adam, which entered the world after its creation, and this argument came to be widely accepted. Thus, Velásquez's painting alludes to Mary's conception in the mind of God from all eternity. Her earthly conception is the earthly realization of this eternal plan.

The painting refers, however, not only to the world's beginning, but also to its end. The young girl visualized here is the Woman of the Apocalypse, 'standing on the moon, clothed with the sun, crowned with stars', and is the mother of the Messiah. In fact, this text is the painting's primary referent, as can be seen from the fact that it has a companion-piece which depicts St John the Divine writing down his revelation on the island of Patmos, and, as he does so, having the vision of the woman of Apocalypse 12. The Woman of the Apocalypse is associated in the text with the overthrowing of the beast – the final defeat of the Devil. Now, because of her Immaculate Conception, Mary is the only human person upon whom the Devil has never had any influence: she is the first, and most perfect, fruit of Christ's conquest over evil, and is thus identified, not only because of her motherhood, but also because of her sinlessness, with the woman of St John's revelation.

This type of iconographic form became enormously popular in the seventeenth century, when it was widely used in churches. Murillo and his school became particularly prolific exponents of the image of the *Immaculada*, and a banner in St Michael's Church, Abertillery, South Wales, incorporates a reproduction of one of Murillo's best-loved paintings of this kind (Figure 16). The Virgin here is dressed in blue and white – the colours which were used by Spanish paintings of the seventeenth century to denote the Immaculate Conception. Previously, Mediterranean artists had most commonly portrayed the Virgin Mary in a red robe and blue mantle; but the modern popularity of the colours blue and white in representations of the Virgin bears witness to the dominance which Immaculate Conception imagery subsequently came to hold in the European religious imagination.

Now, in the Murillo painting reproduced on the banner, the moon on which the Virgin stands is a crescent, but in the painting by Velásquez the moon was a full globe. The crescent is found more commonly than the globe, and, perhaps for that reason, the globe on which the Virgin stood sometimes came to be interpreted as the earth rather than the moon. This interpretation became fixed in Catholic culture with the distribution of the Miraculous Medal and the story of its origin. In 1830, in Paris, a novice religious sister named Catherine Labouré had a series of visions of the Virgin Mary. In one of these, the Virgin instructed her to have a medal struck on this model. The obverse depicts the Virgin Mary standing on a globe. Her hands are outstretched, and lines radiate downwards from the palms. Around the edge of the medal are the words, 'O Mary conceived without sin, pray for us who have recourse to thee.' The Virgin explained to Sister

Figure 16: *Banner of the Immaculate Conception.*
St Michael's Church, Abertillery, South Wales.
Photograph: Martin Crampin.

Catherine that the globe represented the world, but most especially France, and that the lines from the palms of her hands signified God's grace coming down upon it. The text evidently refers to the Immaculate Conception.

The reverse of the medal shows Mary's initial M intertwined with a cross; beneath this, a heart of Jesus is placed next to a heart of Mary; and, around the medal's edge, the twelve stars of the Woman of the Apocalypse provide a frame for the other motifs. The Virgin Mary explained to Sister Catherine that people should wear the medal around their necks. The visionary's spiritual director told the Archbishop of Paris about the visions, and the Archbishop, who was a great supporter of the doctrine of the Immaculate Conception, arranged for the medals to be struck and distributed. The medal was officially entitled the Medal of the Immaculate Conception, but wearers of the medal quickly claimed to have experienced miraculous events which they attributed to the medal's special grace, and so the medal became known as the Miraculous Medal – the name by which millions of Catholics know and wear it today. The image of the Virgin as it appears on the Miraculous Medal was soon copied in other visual arts, and numerous statues of this kind began to appear.

A Miraculous Medal statue at St Non's Well, Pembrokeshire, is evidently the focus of a cult of its own. It always has rosaries hung around it, which must be thank-offerings – probably *ex votos*, or votive offerings, that is, objects brought because the donor has made a vow to make such an offering, or to come on pilgrimage to the shrine, if a particular prayer is granted. They may also represent requests for prayers. Flowers and other objects are also attached to the statue, or left at its feet in the niche. The Virgin stands on a snake. This is a reference to Genesis 3.15, in which God says to the serpent who has led Adam and Eve into disobedience: 'I will place enmity between you and the woman – between your seed and her seed. He will crush your head, and you will bruise his heel.' From early Christian centuries, the designation of the 'woman's seed' as he who would

171

crush the serpent's head was taken as a prophecy of the Incarnation, and the crushed serpent as a prophecy of the Devil's defeat. In the Middle Ages, the image of Mary treading on the serpent became popular, partly because of her part in the Incarnation, but also because it came to be used to signify her Immaculate Conception, since her total freedom from sin is an act and a consequence of the defeat of the Devil, who is signified by the serpent.

This Immaculate Conception iconography is sometimes adapted considerably, as in the wood sculpture by Dorothy Archer (Figure 17) which can be found in St Mary's Church at Betws-y-Coed. Here, the Virgin's hands are turned in in a manner which I am inclined to interpret as a gesture of protection.

Another adaptation of this type of iconography occurs in the popular image of Our Lady of Lourdes. In 1858, a young girl named Bernadette Soubirous had a series of visions of the Virgin Mary in a grotto near Lourdes, a town in the French Pyrenees. Eventually, Bernadette uncovered a healing spring at the site of the apparitions. The lady of the visions identified herself as 'the Immaculate Conception', and the statue of Our Lady of Lourdes is made, as nearly as the artist could manage it, according to the description given by Bernadette herself, including the roses on the Virgin's feet. The site of the apparitions and the spring became – and remains – one of the largest pilgrimage shrines in the world, and Bernadette has been canonized.

In the Catholic church of the Holy Name, Fishguard, a stained-glass window depicts St Bernadette's vision (Plate 12). It is worth noting that the text in the window asks the viewer to 'pray for the donor'. We are not told whether the donor is alive or deceased, but clearly the window is not merely commemorative, but seeks the active response of its audience. In this respect, as well as in its subject matter, the window is distinctively Catholic, and unlike some of the memorial windows in Church in Wales buildings, discussed below. A statue of the generic Lourdes type can be found in the church of Our Lady of

Figure 17: Dorothy Archer, *Mary as Expectant Mother*, wood sculpture.
St Mary's Church, Betws-y-Coed.
Photograph: Martin Crampin.

the Taper (Figure 25, p. 187). Here, the statue of the Virgin forms a pair with one of St Joseph, the two of them flanking a painting of St Michael defeating Satan, the dragon. The motif of conquest over the forces of evil thus appears with particular vividness, and implicitly throws into relief the sinlessness of the Blessed Virgin Mary and associates her with St Michael's victory.

The Annunciation and Incarnation

In churches within the Reformed traditions, images depicting scriptural narratives are of course more common than devotional representations of the Virgin standing alone. In the Church in Wales, the Annunciation (Luke 1.26–38) is, as expected, a common subject for visual representation. The altar frontal at Bistre, in North Wales, is based on a Renaissance model (Plate 13). The three scenes on the Bistre frontal are concerned with the Incarnation. The doctrine that God became human by being conceived in Mary's womb and taking flesh of her flesh is central to the Christian story of salvation, and is at the root of all Marian doctrine and devotion. Because she is the mother of the Word of God – the Son of God, who is the Second Person of the Blessed Trinity – in his humanity, she has the paradoxical title of Mother of God. The Annunciation, to the viewer's right, includes a pillar which divides the heavenly from the earthly. The angel Gabriel moves in front of the pillar, thus indicating the Deity's passing over to be united with the created world in the Incarnation. Gabriel carries a lily, which is traditionally associated with the Virgin Mary, and is commonly shown in Annunciation scenes. The lily is most often said to signify Mary's virginity and purity. Mary herself wears a red robe and blue mantle – a Marian colour-scheme which, as I have observed above, is frequently used by Mediterranean artists of the Middle Ages and Renaissance. Symbolic accounts of Mary's colours usually suggest blue is the colour of heaven, thus indicating her exceptional spiritual qualities, while red is the colour of one of her more earthly attributes, such as compassion or perhaps referring to the Passion of her Son. The angel kneels before the Virgin, acknowledging that he is in the presence of the woman who is uniquely chosen to be the Mother of God. She is, indeed, the Queen of Angels. The placing of a dove in the plasterwork recalls the work of Renaissance artists, and indicates the presence of the Holy Spirit who will come upon Mary.

To the viewer's left is the Visitation of the pregnant Mary to her pregnant cousin Elizabeth (Luke 1.39–56). Elizabeth falls to her knees, apparently crying out, 'And why is this granted me, that the mother of my Lord should come to me?' (v. 43). The central panel shows the Nativity, with Mary kneeling before Christ, who is God incarnate, while Joseph – who is not the child's father, but a witness to the sacred mystery – keeps a respectful distance. The Incarnation makes a particularly good subject for altar decoration, since the function of the altar is the celebration of the Eucharist, and images of the Incarnation serve to remind the worshipper that the body of Christ represented in these scenes is again present in the eucharistic elements.

A similar reminder can be seen in the Lady Chapel reredos at St Mary's Church, Tenby, Pembrokeshire (Figure 18), where the two figures of the Annunciation scene are placed one either side of the central position occupied by the cross. Both figures are kneeling – the angel to the Virgin, and the Virgin before the Holy Spirit, indicated by the dove. The figures here have medieval-style banderoles, or streamers, with texts giving the characters' words. The angel greets the Virgin, and she replies, '*Ecce ancilla Domini*': 'Behold the handmaid of the Lord.'

Another reredos, that at St Mary's Church in Hebrandston in Pembrokeshire, is in more than one respect exceptionally interesting. It is a series of five wooden panels carved in relief, made in 1920 by the ecclesiastical architect John Coates Carter. The two panels on the north side depict the Annunciation and Visitation (Figures 19 and 20);

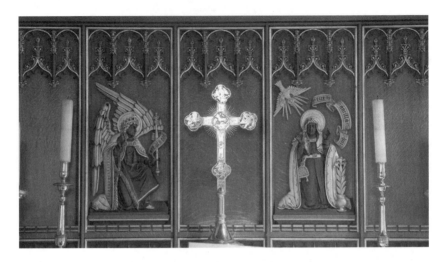

Figure 18: *The Lady Chapel Reredos.* St Mary's Church, Tenby, Pembrokeshire.
Photograph: Martin Crampin.

the central panel shows the Virgin and Child in a mandorla, with the Baptism next to it on the south side (Figure 21); and the final panel depicts the appearance of the risen Christ to his mother (see description of Figure 24 on p. 184).

In the Annunciation scene, Mary is kneeling, reading a book of hours. This is a standard motif in representations of the Annunciation from the later Middle Ages and Renaissance period. A book of hours is a prayer book containing psalms, readings and prayers that are proper to the time of day – Lauds in the morning, Vespers in the evening, and so on. In fact, what these books usually contained was the Little Office of the Blessed Virgin Mary, whose devotions were, as the name suggests, especially in Mary's honour. The origin of these devotions lay in monasteries, but hour books became popular for devotions among middle- and upper-class laity. So Mary is frequently depicted as an aristocratic or bourgeois woman at her devotions. The lily pot is marked with an 'M' for Mary, and the lily blooms are in various stages of blossoming. It is sometimes said that the different

Figure 19: John Coates Carter, *The Annunciation* (1920). St Mary's Church, Hebrandston, Pembrokeshire.
Photograph: Martin Crampin.

Figure 20: John Coates Carter, *The Visitiation* (1920).
St Mary's Church, Hebrandston, Pembrokeshire.
Photograph: Martin Crampin.

Figure 21: John Coates Carter, *Virgin and Child* (1920). St Mary's Church, Hebrandston, Pembrokeshire.
Photograph: Martin Crampin.

stages of blossoming signify Mary's virginity at different stages in her life. Thus, the bloom in bud signifies her virginity before Christ's conception; the bloom that is half-open signifies her virginity even during conception; and the fully flowering lily stands for her continued virginity during childbirth.

The banderole contains Mary's words of assent to Gabriel's message: 'Be it unto me according to thy word.' According to Catholic and Anglican theology, the Incarnation in a certain sense depends upon the free co-operation of the Blessed Virgin Mary. From at least the time of the writings of St Justin Martyr and St Irenaeus in the second century, Christians believed that, when the angel appeared to Mary with the news that she had been chosen to be the mother of the Saviour, God was asking her to give her assent to his will, and that her words, 'Behold the handmaid of the Lord; be it unto me according to thy word', constituted that assent. Without it, God would not have become incarnate as the particular human being whom he was, at the particular time and place at which he did. So the banderole in the Annunciation scene tells the viewer that this is the joyful moment at which God's promise of salvation begins its fulfilment. The Visitation scene (Figure 20), as at Bistre, shows Elizabeth kneeling before Mary. It looks as if this is the moment when Elizabeth prophetically recognizes Mary as the Mother of the Lord; but the text in the banderole is taken from slightly later in Luke's narrative: 'My soul doth magnify the Lord' (Luke 1.46). These, of course, are the opening words of the hymn that Mary proclaims in response to Elizabeth's words, and which are sung every day at Evensong or Vespers. St Mary's Church, Tenby, has a window dedicated to the Magnificat. In this highly original representation of the Visitation, the pregnant Mary is singing her song of rejoicing, with Elizabeth and her husband Zechariah both present and listening. The lily is present around the border, and the vine – which signifies Christ, now present in his mother's womb – fills the background against which the figures stand.

The theology of the Lutheran and, more particularly, Calvinist Reformation emphasizes the fact that all things come from God alone, and is suspicious of attributing any intrinsic worth to human agency. Thus, there is no veneration of the saints in a tradition of this kind, since all good works are due to God alone, and not to the created beings who carry them out. Whereas Catholics would see the veneration of saints as an expression of reverence precisely for God working in and through his creation, classical Protestant theology is wary of such practice, since it seems dangerously close to idolatry. The implication of this view is that Mary's assent is of no theological consequence; all that Mary does is to receive what God has already determined for her. And this indeed seems to be the theological import of this Annunciation scene depicted in the stained-glass window in St Mary's Church, Fishguard. Mary kneels in a manner that has neither joy nor honour about it, in order to receive the heavenly blessing. She kneels like the slave that she proclaims herself to be when she says, 'Behold the handmaid [Greek: *doulē*] of the Lord.' But she seems less like a servant who is honoured and overjoyed to be working for such a noble master, and more like the maidservant in the psalm, who watches in subjection for the hand of her mistress.

The last Annunciation scene to be considered is that which flanks an image of Our Lady of Pity, or the *Pietà*, on the reredos of the Lady altar in the church of St John the Baptist, Newport, South Wales (Figure 22). It was made by A. R. Henderson in 1939, and is a fine piece of work in a style that might be described as 'sub-Giotto'. The central panel shows Our Lady of Pity: that is, the dead Christ being held by his mother – a subject that is artistically very tricky, since it requires depicting the body of an adult man lying across the lap of a woman. Beneath Our Lady of Pity, on the altar frontal, is a painting of the Virgin and Child. It was once common to pair these two images with one another, partly because of the visual parallel between the mother holding her infant son and the mother holding her adult son, but also because of a theological correspondence between the two. The image of the Virgin and Child depicts Christ as the infant who was born from his mother in order to die for the world, while Our

179

Lady of Pity shows the dead Christ whose death is a preparation for new life, or re-birth. So each image recalls and informs the other.

The Annunciation figures are placed one either side of the *Pietà*, with the Virgin seated. This precise arrangement is unusual, but the juxtaposition of the *Pietà* and the Annunciation reinforces the symbolism that I have referred to above, since Christ's conception as a human being led inevitably to death, but that death in turn made possible new life. The scriptural quotation beneath the reredos is from Luke 1: *Magnificat anima mea dominum* – 'My soul doth magnify the Lord'; but the paintings are better read as a reminder of John 16.21: 'When a woman is in travail she has sorrow, because her hour has come; but when she is delivered of the child, she no longer remembers the anguish, for joy that a human being is born into the world.' Christ speaks these words as a prophecy of the new life that will emerge from the sorrow of his Passion (v. 22).

The suffering of Christ and his mother

Representations of Mary's presence at her Son's Passion appear in both Catholic and Anglican churches, although, as with many other types of representation, they are less obviously a focus of devotion for Anglicans than they are for Catholics.

At the church of Our Lady Queen of Peace at Newcastle Emlyn, West Wales, an enormous rood scene stands outside, on top of the porch, apparently as a public proclamation of faith. Inside the church, there is a piece of sculpture of a very different style: a youthful Virgin holds the infant Christ in a standing posture in her hands, with his own arms extended so that he forms the shape of a cross. The figure reminds the viewer that Christ was born into the world in order to die for it, and Catholics often comment that Christ's outstretched arms signify his embracing of the whole world. The figure of the Virgin with the cruciform child has become very popular in the last few decades,

Figure 22: A. R. Henderson, *Pietà* (1939). Church of St John the Baptist, Newport, South Wales.
Photograph: Martin Crampin.

being found in domestic, ecclesiastical and monumental settings. Also at the Catholic church in Newcastle Emlyn, there is a grotto in which another standing Virgin holds the Christ-child with his arms out-stretched, although here the gesture may perhaps be more one of welcome than of anticipated suffering.

A particularly fine example of this general type, however, is the Virgin and Child from the church of the Most Holy Redeemer, Porthmadog. It seems to be carved from stone, and is a figure of considerable iconographic clarity. It is good as sacred art because it is concerned only with sacred meaning and sentiment, and not with attempts at realism or with mundane emotion.

More similar to the figure from the grotto at Newcastle Emlyn is the statue in the Lady Chapel at the church of Our Lady of Sorrows, Dolgellau (Figure 23). The architectural style is mock Romanesque, and it was constructed by local people out of local materials. The church also contains a painting of the church's patron saint by Powys Evans, a local artist who based the work on a painting in Bruges. It shows Our Lady of Sorrows surrounded by scenes depicting her seven sorrows. Meditation on the sorrows of the Virgin has been a part of Catholic practice since the Middle Ages, although the number and identity of the sorrows has varied in different traditions. In the four-teenth century, the Servite Order promoted devotion to a particular set of seven sorrows, and this set became more or less standard across the Catholic world. It is these seven sorrows which are depicted in Powys Evans' painting. Starting at the bottom left, and moving round clock-wise, they are: Simeon's prophecy that a sword would pierce Mary's soul (Luke 2.35); the flight into Egypt (Matthew 2.13–15); the losing of Christ in the Temple (Luke 2.41–45); Christ carrying the cross; the Crucifixion; the deposition from the cross; and Christ's entombment. In much devotional art – especially that of Hispanic countries – Our Lady of Sorrows is depicted as having an agonized face, with a sword (or seven swords – one for each of the sorrows) piercing her breast. Here, however, she is sombre and restrained.

Figure 23: *Statue of the Virgin.* Church of Our Lady of Sorrows, Dolgellau.
Photograph: Martin Crampin.

The Resurrection

Following Christ's burial, of course, comes his Resurrection. And it is at this point that we find what is truly the most surprising of Marian images in Welsh churches, namely, the appearance of the risen Christ to his mother, on the Carter reredos at St Mary's Church, Hebrandston (Figure 24). This scene is not described in Scripture, and it is very unusual to find it represented in recent art – especially in an Anglican church.

From at least as early as the fourth century, it was widely believed that Christ's first Resurrection appearance was to his mother (perhaps because of a confusion between the Virgin Mary and St Mary Magdalene), and this belief continued in the Catholic Church until the early modern period, and is still widely held among the

Figure 24: John Coates Carter, *Appearance of the Risen Christ to his Mother.*
St Mary's Church, Hebrandston, Pembrokeshire.
Photograph: Martin Crampin.

Eastern Orthodox. St Ignatius of Loyola points out that, according to the Book of Acts, Christ appeared to many people, and there is every reason to suppose that one of these would have been his mother. Nevertheless, the image of a Resurrection appearance to the Virgin Mary can cause considerable consternation among Christians of the modern West. In the stained glass of St Lawrence's Church, Ludlow, a late medieval depiction of the Resurrection to the Virgin Mary is recorded in the church guide book as the Resurrection to St Mary Magdalene. The depiction that is probably of more significance for the relief at Hebrandston, however, is that in the famous fifteenth-century stained glass at Fairford Church, Gloucestershire, where the subject of the scene is not contested. In the representation at Fairford, the Virgin kneels at a prie-Dieu, as she does at Hebrandston, and it seems reasonable to suppose that Fairford provided the model for Carter's carving.

The reredos at Hebrandston is marked with the remarkable words, 'A thank offering for the safe return of all the men of the parish from the Great War 1914–18', and perhaps it is not too fanciful to suppose that the motif of Christ's appearance to his mother was chosen as especially suitable for such a thanksgiving: for how many mothers in Hebrandston must have felt that their sons were indeed returning from the dead?

Images of Mary distinctive to Wales

At this point, we leave the narratives of Scripture, and turn to Welsh folklore. Medieval Wales was home to many popular shrines of the Virgin Mary, the most important of which was probably that of Penrhys, Glamorganshire. The one which the present-day Roman Catholic Church designates as the National Shrine, however, is that of Our Lady of the Taper, at Cardigan. The original site of the shrine is the Anglican, former priory, church of St Mary, on the banks of the

River Teifi. According to tradition, a statue of the Virgin and Child was washed up on the shore here, and in the Virgin's hand was a lighted taper which burned continuously without melting away. A chapel was built to house the statue with its miraculous taper, but, after nine years, a man broke an oath which he had sworn upon it, and the flame went out. Our Lady of the Taper remained a popular object of devotion and pilgrimage until Henry VIII's destruction of the shrines, and it is possible that the devotion survived until the reign of Elizabeth I.

The Catholic Church has built a new shrine of Our Lady of the Taper, with a bronze statue, cast by Mother Concordia (Figure 25) and based upon the Medieval Virgin in Majesty, or Seat of Wisdom. Although the legend of the taper is not biblical, the story's imagery of water and light has strong biblical resonances. In Genesis 1.1–3, the world is first made as a watery mass, and God's first work of creation is the making of light. The images of the taper and the water appear in both stained glass and textile art in Our Lady's Church, and devotions at the shrine focus upon Christ as the Light of the World (John 1.4–5). We might also remember that the element of water and the light and warmth of the sun are the foundation and sustenance of human physical life and of the earth itself.

The throne of Our Lady of the Taper is decorated with images of flowers that are named in Welsh for the Virgin Mary. *Tapr Mair*, for example – literally, 'Mary's taper' – is the flower known most commonly in English as Aaron's rod. Marian flower names are found all across Europe. In England, for example, we have the lady's slipper orchid ('Our Lady's slipper'), the marigold ('Mary's gold'), or lady's bower (clematis). Welsh seems to be particularly rich in such names, and several Welsh churches incorporate representations of these flowers in their decoration. At the shrine of Our Lady of the Taper, for the inauguration of the chapel at Cardigan as the Welsh National Shrine, a taper was placed in the hand of the shrine statue and lit at Pentecost, 1986. The candle had been blessed by Pope John Paul II,

Figure 25: Mother Concordia, *Our Lady of the Taper.* Cardigan, mid-Wales.
Photograph: Martin Crampin.

and it is now housed in a wooden casket made by Harry Comley, decorated with relief carvings of Marian flowers. In addition to the art-work in the shrine chapel, the church at Cardigan has a fine set of stained-glass windows depicting Marian flowers, made by Amber Hiscott. Anglican churches have likewise made use of Marian flowers in their decoration. St Saviour's Church, Splott (Cardiff), has Marian flower motifs set in relief on the wall either side of the tabernacle. And St David's Church, Llanfaes, has an altar frontal with an embroidered wheel of such flowers. Perhaps the most prominent example is the Lady Chapel reredos at Llandaff Cathedral, designed and made by Frank Roper.

Of the many recent Marian representations in Wales, my own favourite is also one that associates Mary with the natural world. This is a window that was formerly in the Catholic church of Mair y Coed ('St Mary of the Woods') at Betws-y-Coed (mid-Wales), and it shows the Virgin and Child in woodland. Its original setting was the church porch, where it welcomed visitors to a place of prayer in the midst of woods, mountains and streams. The church at Betws was closed, and the window is now in the Lady Chapel of the Catholic church at the nearby town of Llanrwst. Like the Virgin of the Immaculate Conception, who, as Holy Wisdom, speaks of God's creation of the universe, Our Lady of the Taper and Mair y Coed remind the devotee that the God who became incarnate in Mary's womb is present in all times and places, and they continue to call the worshipper to honour God's presence in both art and nature.

Suggested reading

Sarah Boss, *Empress and Handmaid: Nature and Gender in the Cult of the Virgin Mary* (London: Cassell, 1999).

Sally Cunneen, *In Search of Mary* (New York: Ballantine Books, 1996).

Jaroslav Pelikan, *Mary Through the Centuries* (New Haven: Yale University Press, 1996).

10

Hermeneutics, aesthetics and transcendence

NICHOLAS DAVEY

In what sense can a biblical painting draw the viewer into the biblical narrative? Nicholas Davey examines, from the point of view of the philosopher, the process that takes place when we engage with a work of art, in this case a biblical painting. Basing his argument on the work of Hans-Georg Gadamer, he shows how a painting reveals new aspects each time we view it, allowing us to interpret the biblical story depicted in new and unexpected ways.

Introduction

The question I wish to address is as follows: can art both in the broad sense of creative endeavour and in the more narrow sense of the visual arts illuminate our understanding of revelation and transcendence? I believe that art does afford such an understanding, not because it describes or illustrates revelation and transcendence but because aesthetic experience attests to them. In the terms of Hans-Georg Gadamer, it is because art 'addresses' us, it is because of what happens to us in the course of and as a consequence of this address, that our experience of being so spoken to offers an insight into the phenomenological nature of revelation and transcendence. Gadamer argues:

> An artwork 'says something to someone.' In this assertion is
> contained the dismay of finding oneself directly affected by
> what was said by the work, and being forced to reflect again
> and again on what was said there, in order to make it under-
> standable to oneself and to others. I therefore continue to
> maintain that the experience of art is an experience of
> meaning.[1]

There is no incongruity in talking of art, hermeneutics and the Bible.
Gadamer's hermeneutics is not concerned with translating literary experience into visual experience or vice versa. It recognizes that the Bible
and art communicate as modes of language that deploy signs and
symbols in analogous ways. As visual and literary modes of communication, their respective signs and symbols refer to and evoke the same
subject matters: questions of mystery, of the ineffable, of eternal
renewal. Each approach opens a different perspective for the other with
regard to the common subject matter and in so doing can transform the
possibilities that the other sees in such subject matter. Returning to the
point, however, my interest in revelation and transcendence is not
merely an interest in two objects that actualize themselves within experience. It is rather that a phenomenological approach to these
essences or entities discloses something of the intricate connections
between hermeneutics, aesthetics and religion. My thesis is that if we
can understand something of the hermeneutic content of aesthetic experience, we can understand an aspect of the transcendent as given with
religious experience. To illuminate my suggestion I shall need to specify
my terms somewhat.

Hermeneutics

Hermeneutics has traditionally been associated with the rules and
methods of textual interpretation. The roots of the discipline stretch

back to the study and the illumination of Jewish and Christian Holy Scripture. Hermeneutics has in consequence often been presented as a tool box for theological and literary criticism, supplying means for the interpreter to impose or recover anticipated meanings from a text. Recent theories of interpretation have been sensitive to what Nietzsche described as a will to power, a tendency of interpretive stratagems to impose their own advantageous assumptions upon a text. Heidegger sought to reverse such methodological subjectivism by allowing the text to speak for itself and, thereby, to challenge the initial expectancies of a reader. Gadamer does not subject the text to interpretive methods either but seeks to subject the reader to being questioned by the text. Heidegger and Gadamer are deeply sceptical of Dilthey's methodological hermeneutics. Dilthey's investigation into the human world was much like the Elizabethan philosopher Francis Bacon's (1561–1623) enquiry into the natural world: phenomena are subject to the 'rack' of method until they confess their hidden truths. To escape the connotations of a will to power (subjectivism) within modern literary and theological hermeneutics, Heidegger's ontological approach to hermeneutics reverses the dynamic of subjection. Heidegger and Gadamer tend to malign Dilthey as a hermeneutical Bacon. His methodological hermeneutics is caricatured as a process whereby a reader, in order to force a text to give up its inner truth, *subjects* it to the tortuous machines of interpretation. In Heidegger's thought it is the reader who is subjected to what bursts forth from within the text and often, as Gadamer points out, contrary to his or her willing and doing. Within this framework of reasoning, reading is submissive. It involves an opening towards, a preparation for an annunciative event, an epiphanic moment in which something from within the text discloses itself. The sense of hermeneutics here is Gadamerian. The object of attention is not a body of rules governing both the interpretation and the commentary of texts or paintings, but concerned with articulating *how* and *under what conditions* what comes forth in the event of looking and reading discloses itself:

> There is no hermeneutic method . . . Hermeneutics means not
> so much a procedure as the attitude of a person who wants to
> understand someone else . . . An interpreter who really has
> mastered scholarly methods uses them only so that the experi-
> ence of the poem becomes possible through better understand-
> ing.[2]

Gadamer's hermeneutics is not a discourse theory: it does not claim,
as Derrida does, that there is no outside or beyond a text. To the
contrary, Gadamer's hermeneutics attests to an experience of that
which, though given to the eye in a text or painting, always reaches
beyond to that which is not obviously seen or stated. Hermeneutics,
whether literary or visual, concerns itself with bringing to light what
is hidden or with uncovering that which is not straightforwardly seen
in a work. It is tempting, here, to think of palimpsests and *pentimenti*,
tempting because Gadamerian hermeneutics does indeed concern itself
with animating the presence of what is hidden.[3] Yet this is a temptation to be resisted. Palimpsests and *pentimenti* imply a lost truth, an
original overlaid and disguised, but nevertheless present, there, below
the surface, awaiting recovery by the loyal and the faithful. However,
Gadamerian hermeneutics neither rests on nor promotes such assumptions. Gadamer is unequivocally postmodern in this respect. He flatly
rejects archaeological models of interpretation: there is no first word
to be recovered that will redeem all subsequent words and give them
their final meaning.

Despite such Nietzschean dimensions, Gadamer's thinking is firmly
committed not to a *truth* that has been withheld but, rather, as we
shall see, to the truth of *withheldness* itself. Indeed, Gadamer's
thought is fundamentally preoccupied with the aesthetic and spiritual
resonances of the *truth* of withheldness. What is meant by recovering
a sense of the hidden?

What a text or a painting shows or reveals is not an image of the
actual world in any simple sense of the relationship between an

original and its image. A work can give rise to, bring to mind and re-acquaint us with a life world, a mode of being that shows itself to have been at work in shaping the outlook of both reader and writer or painter. Robert Pippin puts it accurately when he speaks of aesthetics and hermeneutical experience attesting to what shows itself in a text or a painting: namely, that world which reveals itself as having *already* been at work shaping the pre-reflective engagements which constitute the circuitries of meanings and commitments that establish the background 'for-the-sake-of-which' that governs our actions. Gadamerian hermeneutics endeavours not so much to recover, let alone re-appropriate, the withheld but to be inflected by its workings. How is this ontologically nuanced approached to hermeneutics related to aesthetics?

Aesthetics

Though its importance is still not fully appreciated, Heidegger and Gadamer effect a sea-change in aesthetic thought. Both thinkers strive to overcome the subjectivist connotations of post-Kantian aesthetics. They rigorously oppose the convictions that judgements of taste are rooted in the preferences, inclinations and actions of the perceiving subject. Aesthetic experience is the experience of something acting on us contrary to our willing and doing. In other words, aesthetic experience is annunciative, an event to which we are subject. The suggestion here is not only that the event of aesthetic experience is ontological – a moment and an expression of *being* – but also that such experience is the occasion of something revealing itself. Aesthetics in the hands of Heidegger and Gadamer is *epiphanic*, a process whereby something shows itself. We should make it clear that we are not concerned with the representations of the vague and the indistinct.

Though Heidegger was much taken by the brushwork of Japanese watercolours, it is not misty images of flow and flux that are relevant, for they indicate a *representational* aesthetic: i.e. they re-present (refer to) something exterior to the painting, perhaps even seek to stabilize it. Gadamer's aesthetics are, by contrast, presentational (*darstellen*): aesthetic experience is the occasion of something presenting itself from within an experience of a work. In Gadamer's phrase, something comes into picture, something is figured from within its borders. His paradigm is religious art. There can be no picture (portrait) of the face of God but, rather, what comes into picture is the divine configured as a face that addresses us. However, without anticipating too much of the later discussion, the question of *what* is figured within the picture invites two responses.

First: what is brought to mind is exactly the *Lebenswelt* that Pippin talks of, that is, that nexus of associations, meanings and insights that constitutes the horizon of our actions and commitments but which nevertheless transcends them. Second: what is brought to mind can also be described as the *Sachen* – the subject matters, the *foci* of concerns, which constitute such a *Lebenswelt*. Subject matters might be described as the living tissues of human existence: they can concern redemption, love, transcendence, loyalty and precariousness. They show themselves in manifolds of appearance. Their presence in an artwork can operate effectively as a symbol.

Unlike a sign that forever defers to an external meaning that it points to, symbols are not self-negating. They are the presence of their meaning, the material site in and through which its meaning shows itself. However, the meaning that appears never appears *in totum*: it is always more, always something withheld. It is in this conjunction that it is possible to speak of the *excess*, to speak of the *transcendent* in art. In summary, the connection between hermeneutics and aesthetics is ontological. Hermeneutics is concerned with understanding the epiphany of meaning within a text or painting. Hermeneutical aesthetics is primarily concerned with what a work of art shows, with what it brings into appearance in the phenomenological sense of the term.

And so, to sum up: by hermeneutical, I allude to that which is hidden and by aesthetic I refer to a mode of appearing. *Hermeneutical aesthetics points to the appearing of the hidden, the hidden making itself manifest.* I shall argue that such a conception of hermeneutical aesthetics makes it a natural ally of certain conceptions of the transcendent. What then of the relationship between hermeneutics and theology? The link concerns the aesthetic once again.

Theology

Modern hermeneutics has a long association with theology and biblical exegesis. Questions of interpretive method were of strategic importance to the Protestant reform movement. *Sola scriptura* – 'only the Scriptures' – was the rallying cry of those reformers who resisted Catholic institutionalized religious practices on the grounds that their origin lay in the arbitrary conventions of the human world and not in the divine 'word' of the Bible. In philosophy, Gadamer's concern with meaning and tradition has fostered a conservative image of his work. One does not customarily think of Gadamer as a postmodernist. However, this is not so in recent theological debate.

Gadamer is too close to Nietzsche not to be sensitive to the fact that the reformist commitment to *sola scriptura* led to a massive epistemological crisis which, because of a general failure to agree on the nature and authority of linguistic meaning, promoted the eclipse of the very notion of Scripture itself. As Valentine Cunningham argues, 'reading always comes after'. No one ever did read in a completely new way for all reading is schooled by anticipations of what a text or what a meaning is.[4] The Protestant notion of 'reading alone' is enabled paradoxically by the very Catholic insight that it resisted, namely that in historical actuality one is never alone with the word. The solo reader is in practice already armed with a panoply of socially acquired interpretive rules. His or her reading is possible only because of the 'all too human', and therefore ever re-negotiable, hermeneutic practices of institutionally established communication and decipherment.

The postmodernist thinker might ask, 'Is this the road to the abyss of postponement and deferment?' As Foucault suggests, does not such an account of interpretation doom us to an endless task because it rests on the postulate that speech is an act of translation, an exegesis which listens to the word of God, ever secret, ever beyond itself? Are we not condemned to wait in vain for the decision of the Word? Gadamer shares with Foucault a deep scepticism of the very critical attitude that first Protestantism and then the Enlightenment nurtured: the centring of authority in a rational self. Yet Gadamer's demystification of reason and religion leads in an altogether different direction from that of Foucault.

Gadamer appreciated personally what was at issue in Bultmann's project. Bultmann's *Demythologization of the New Testament* is according to Gadamer a provocative working out of an exegetical procedure he had always followed: 'It was a formulation of the hermeneutical principle that understanding must be a translation into one's own language if it is to be real understanding.'[5]

The reference is of course metaphorical: it must be a translation into what makes sense for me, into what addresses me, but this does not necessarily involve a translation into one's own tongue. Gadamer's 'phenomenological reduction' of the religious is part of the mythopoietic reversal at the core of his hermeneutics. What concerns Gadamerian thought about the *human* words of the Christ and the Buddha is what they *attest* to, that is, decidedly not to faith and dogma but to certain *spiritual* truths which concern the experience of human limitation and weakness, the illusion of individual independence or the longing or need for recognition by an other:

The principle upon which (such) understanding is based is that of reversal. What is presented as the action and suffering of others is understood as the experience of one's own suffering. Even the concept of 'demythologizing' . . . implies the principal of this reversal, to the extent that the meaning of religious proclamation in the New Testament is limited by this reversal to a human understanding of faith.[6]

Gadamer's stance entails a phenomenology not of something named as religion but of experience with a religious connotation: that is, of experiences of that otherness that limit or define us as human beings. The equation between religion and limit experiences is quite plain.

'learning through suffering' . . . What a man (or woman) has to learn through suffering is not this or that particular thing, but insight into the limitations of humanity, into the absoluteness of the barrier man from the divine. It is ultimately a religious insight.[7]

Three things are apparent here: (a) experience is central, the key experience being the moment when a person becomes insightful; (b) the 'religious' or 'spiritual' element within experience does not concern a specific object of such experience but rather a certain form of experience, a form which is invariably double, both centrifugal and centripetal. Spiritual truths, whether they are to do with love, with death or with the foibles of the individual, are on the one hand ecstatic and centrifugal (we are suddenly brought to see the hugeness of what lies beyond our immediate horizon). On the other hand they are centripetal: highly individualizing, locating us very firmly within our immediate circumstances. The enormity of what is entailed in love or death does not really make itself apparent until I fall in love or I lose someone dear to me. (c) Spiritual experience is thus essentially an experience of a certain movement or journeying. Such reflective experience has life and movement. Gadamer also states, 'The essence of what is called spirit lies in the ability to move within the horizon of an open future and an unrepeatable past.' The 'moving on' which is characteristic of spiritual well-being often happens to us contrary to our willing and doing. Hermeneutic experience is an experience of *passio, of something revealing itself to us in those quiet moments of reading or looking.*

The simultaneously dislocating and relocating nature of spiritual experience lends something of the symbolic to it. A symbol never reveals all of its facets: the finitude of both human experience and of a symbol reveals itself, always means that there is always more to be said. Both bring us into the presence of an unarticulated excess. We shall return to the importance of the symbol in our discussion of hermeneutical aesthetics below. However, the range and variety of interpretation associated with the symbol brings us back to the links between Gadamer's hermeneutics and postmodern theology.

Gadamer's thought has a distinctly postmodern tone to it in that it insists that all reading subjects acknowledge their own situatedness and interestedness. This is not to relativize our readings, for all reading is never *solo scriptura*. Reading, like understanding, is not to be thought of as a subjective act but involves participation in distinct traditions. Gadamer's thought brings to an end that opposition between the alleged purity of privileged conscientious reading and the institutional interests of traditional religious bodies. Tradition in the broader sense of a historical and intellectual horizon is re-appropriated as a precondition of reading.

This is not a relativism. The argument is not that we can *only* speak within our tradition. A tradition may, over time, acquire shared subject matters but this does not mean that the *view* of such subject matters is shared. To the contrary, the fact that there are different views of the same subject matter is why Gadamer grasps all tradition as dialogical. Dialogical exchange not only recognizes the perspectival nature of tradition but renews and sustains it. The theologian Dan Stiver sums up eloquently:

(The) capacity for encounter across horizons is also a counter-
balance to the emphasis upon the situatedness of every
theology. While one's location should be considered a strength
as well as an unavoidable reality, we have obligation to
dialogue with (other) theologies . . . Absolute agreement on all
matters is neither likely nor desirable but one's situated
theology can only be strengthened by the (dialogical) attempt
to do justice to other perspectives.[8]

Far from being a conservative voice in theology, Gadamer's hermeneutics has contributed to its phenomenological renaissance. Postmodern
thought addresses the endless text and acknowledges the absence of
any end-station for interpretation. As we shall see, these features are
for Gadamer integral to an aesthetic experience of the symbol itself.

Gadamer and religious experience

In order to bring the three elements of my discussion together, I shall
dwell on that aspect of Gadamer's account of religious experience
which concerns transcendence. This will provide an important link
with the final part of our discussion concerning a religious dimension
of aesthetic experience. What is meant in the present context by transcendence does not involve reference to something extra-experiential,
to an entity beyond the bounds of present experience. Transcendence,
to the contrary, is inherent within experience, part of its very topog-
raphy. When transcendence is discussed, Gadamer speaks of a process
whereby, in coming to know something more intimately, we realize
both the shallowness of our former experience and the extent to which
the horizons of that more intimate experience now expand so as to
reveal in that order of experience more dimensions than we ever
imagined were initially present. A deepening experience of a subject
matter, a re-reading of a book, looking at a painting for the second or

third time, involves an experience of transcendence in that we come to see in what we overlooked, our former blindness, and the shallowness of our former judgement. Yet, at the same time, we marvel at what now shows itself to us and are enlivened by the life-quickening expectancy of more to see or more to understand. This is an experience of transcendence in that it changes our sense of self by expanding its possibilities, reveals the limits of its understanding and shows *that our understanding and sense of self is utterly dependent upon that which transcends our individual being.* Transcendence speaks of those 'supra-individual ontological realities' which reach beyond and yet shape individual consciousness.

Existence is a *mysterium*, a matter of mystery. Its riddles are not problems that can be solved. To the contrary, all mysteries can only be better appreciated and understood more profoundly. Language and history too are *mysteriums*. As such, our being is utterly dependent on that full nature which lies well beyond our grasp. Our being is in a very real sense *upheld* by that which is withheld. The withheld is simultaneously present within experience and yet transcends it. An experience of transcendence is thus centrifugal and centripetal. It discloses how human experience is bounded, shaped and limited by what it cannot grasp, albeit that it remains utterly dependent upon what it cannot grasp. However, though the transcendent which limits human understanding may surpass understanding, it does not surpass *all* understanding, as we shall see. Nevertheless, the key point remains. Speaking of Karl Jaspers, Jürgen Habermas remarks:

> One's own existence cannot be illuminated without an enlightened account of 'transcendence'. This is Jaspers' name for that which always sustains and encompasses us. This all-embracing reality (*das Umgreifende*) is another expression for the horizon of the linguistically structured life world, within which we already find ourselves.[9]

For the self to be aware of the transcendent is for the self to be aware both of something that bears the marks of otherness and that otherness is (insofar as it is linguistic) an otherness within the self. From this demythologized and quite accessible notion of transcendence, let me move towards a summary of the connections and then to my final comments.

Towards an aesthetic of the withheld

> Darkness itself comes to light, as much as it can in philosophy, but philosophy must have the good sense to let the darkness be.[10]

Let me pose a question. How can that which transcends experience and how can the presence of that which is not visible be discerned? How can we behold that which is withheld? Our conclusion offers a response to this question. The response entails grasping the poignant inter-connections of vital aspects of hermeneutics, theology and aesthetics. Sokolowski is one of those rare and brave philosophers who acknowledge that philosophy has neglected to its cost the vague, the obscure and the hidden. 'There would be no philosophy if we were incapable of attaining some truth but it is also the case that there would be no philosophy, no search for wisdom . . . if there were no ignorance, no hiddenness, no vagueness . . .'[11] Sokolowski and other thinkers who defend the hidden and obscure are *not* arguing for the duality of light and dark. The truth as truth is always accompanied by its shadow: 'Any truth that we achieve is always surrounded by absence and hiddenness, by *mystery,* since the thing we know is always more than we can know, the reference is always more than the sense.'[12]

These remarks are historically neither arbitrary nor isolated. To the contrary, as we shall see, they attest to the fact that the notion of the withheld is at the heart of the phenomenological mode of thought defended by Heidegger and Gadamer. In approaching the notion of the withheld, Gadamer remarks that:

> No one can ignore the fact that in the work of art, in which a world arises, not only is something meaningful given to experience that was not known before, but also something new comes into existence with the work of art itself. It is not simply the laying bare of a truth, it is itself an event.[13]

In 'speaking to us' an art work 'brings something forth from uncon-cealedness' but 'the emergence into light' is not the annihilation of concealedness *per se* but the revelation of *a continued sheltering in the dark*. He further remarks:

> There is clearly a tension between the emergence and the sheltering that constitutes . . . a work of art and produces the brilliance by which it outshines everything else. Its truth is not constituted simply by its laying bare its meaning but rather by the unfathomable depth of its meaning. Thus by its very nature the work of art is a conflict between . . . emergence and sheltering.[14]

Disclosure and hiddenness are, therefore, not mutually exclusive. That an aspect of a work's content comes forward also reveals the extent to which much of its content does not, and remains undisclosed. The suggestiveness and speculative charge of a work resides in the fact that, alluringly, they hold themselves back exactly because they come forward into the openness of presence. The enigmatic nature of art-works does not involve their intelligible dimensions being pitted against their mysterious aspects. It is precisely the disclosed aspects which render a work intelligible and in turn reveal the presence of its unseen elements. In his aesthetics, the French theologian Maritain speaks of how 'things are not only what they are' but also of how 'they give more than they have'. For our purposes, the withheld is an extremely poignant notion. Consider the following.

The excess within the withheld is (a) that which escapes present interpretation. It serves as the hermeneutic foundation of the always-more-to-be-said, the basis of all future interpretation. The withheld is the guarantee of future learning and understanding. The excess within the withheld is (b) the ontological basis of the possibility of transcendence. It is the condition of transformative experience. In it lies the possibility of the always more to be understood and it is such excess which challenges and limits the scope of our present understanding. An encounter with the withheld is intimately connected with the experience of limit which Gadamer associates with (his phenomenological) conception of religious experience. The excess within the withheld is (c) that which enables symbols to function. Symbols show a meaning but they never exhaust that meaning. Its explicit finite meaning invokes what it stands on, an infinity of unstated meaning. The symbol has a sensory meaning but its function is to bring forth the presence of the non-sensory meaning which only the sensory makes discernible. Within aesthetic experience, symbols function, if I may borrow an astronomical term, as 'wormholes' of the transcendent. They both open a portal to that infinity of meaning which transcends and yet sustains any given symbol or work, and establish a portal through which such an infinity can disclose (albeit partially) its presence. The excess within the withheld is (d) that which not only provides a basis for articulating for the capacity of art-works to transcend their epoch but also to offer an understanding of why some works go into eclipse. As Sokolowski observes, 'Hiddenness is not just loss: it can also be preservation and protection. Things need their right time to be seen . . . may be waiting for the right moment to be understood . . . Concealment is also preservation.'[15]

In addition to the above and by way of bringing this chapter to a conclusion, I would argue that the withheld has a double character

205

within hermeneutical aesthetics. The first aspect is that the withheld has no presence in aesthetics unless some aspect of what was formerly hidden is now, presently, revealed. This is consistent with our claim that hermeneutical aesthetics is concerned with the coming into appearance of that which was hidden though evidently operative in our thinking, feeling and seeing. Aesthetic experience is revered as an occasion in which the background world that is our culture, a world which, like language, is for the most part taken for granted and is perhaps even more efficacious because of such forgetfulness, is brought to light, remembered and shown to have been operative in our willing and doing. Art thereby occupies a privileged role for Heidegger and Gadamer. It opens a space freed from the concerns of the pragmatic and the utilitarian in which the world, which always did transcend the knowing subject, comes to light. The emergence of such a world, the changes in understanding that it initiates and the expanded vision it enables, are central to both Gadamer's phenomenological treatment of the transcendent and his particular grasp of the nature of spiritual insight. However, there is a second face to the withheld which is in certain ways much more profound.

I argued above that Gadamer is concerned with the truth of withheldness as such. It is true that the withheld has no presence in aesthetics unless some aspect of what was formerly hidden is now presently revealed. But this is only half the argument. The revelation of what was formerly hidden is also *a revelation of the continued presence of that which continues to be hidden*. Disclosure is not just a discontinued hiddenness but a revelation of continued concealment. In being more than itself, any symbol is also the presence of what is excess, of what is not yet said. But what remains concealed is not another order of Being. It is *this* being but in its hermeneutical totality – which is to say that it is the very *otherness* of this being, that which is beyond our grasp, beyond being stateable and yet always effectively present. The withheld, if I might put it this way, is not *not*. It is not the equivalent of a *deus absconditas*, a hidden God, but closer, perhaps, to a *theological negative*. The withheld may be concealed from understanding but it always upholds understanding.

Though no word can capture the totality of meaning that under-writes it, though no symbol can exhaust the meaning it makes present and though no theory can completely grasp the complexity of horizons which informs a cultural practice, all are dependent upon what transcends them. *They are all truly upheld by the withheld.* Here the German for the withheld and hidden – *Verber-gung* – reveals its own extraordinary resonance. The word is con-nected to *Berg,* poignant with its suggestion of the mountainous, of dense, rock-like sustaining support. This second sense of the withheld concerns that which upholds our linguistic and cultural being. It is immanent in all that we do and think and yet cannot be circumscribed by any action and thought. It is not a piece of mysti-fication in that those aspects of itself that are disclosed are disclosed in the intelligible languages of both sign and symbol. Yet it remains a mystery in that it can only ever be attested to. The withheld is the truth of transcendence, a truth which is attested to by the hermeneu-tic dimensions of all art, a truth which has an undeniable spiritual if not religious dimension. The truth is that as linguistic and cultural beings we are indeed dependent upon those supra-individual onto-logical actualities which inform and yet transcend our being. We are, in thought, word and deed, upheld by the withheld. It is the hermeneutic truth of revelation and transcendence that both our experience of art and the Bible can so brilliantly disclose.

Notes

1 Hans-Georg Gadamer, *Gadamer in Conversation, Reflections and Com-mentary*, ed. R. E. Palmer (New Haven: Yale University Press, 2001), p. 70.

2 Hans-Georg Gadamer, *Gadamer on Celan, 'Am I and Who Are You?'* (Albany: State University of New York, 1993), p. 161.

3   A palimpsest is a document that has been written over another, an image that is poignant for hermeneutics in that one thinker's position is often regarded as a re-working of another's. Hermeneutics has often been characterized as that mode of reading which seeks to determine the arguments that underlie those that appear on a page. Not so in the case of Gadamer, who thinks of the differences between original and copy as themselves expanding on a shared subject matter. *Pentimento* refers to the process whereby an artist 'repents' from what he has painted and over-paints a canvas. The hidden image is occasionally presented as the 'original' which interpretation must recover.

4   Valentine Cunningham, *Reading After Theory* (Oxford: Blackwell, 2002), pp. 7–11.

5   Hans-Georg Gadamer, *Philosophical Apprenticeships* (Cambridge, MA: MIT Press, 1985), p. 59.

6   Hans-Georg Gadamer, *Literature and Philosophy in Dialogue* (Albany: State University of New York Press, 1994), p. 159.

7   Hans-Georg Gadamer, *Truth and Method* (London: Sheed and Ward, 1989), p. 357.

8   Dan R. Stiver, 'Theological Method' in *The Cambridge Companion to Post-Modern Theology* (Cambridge: Cambridge University Press, 2003), p. 180.

9   Jürgen Habermas, *The Liberating Power of Symbols, Philosophical Essays* (London: Polity, 2001), p. 38.

10 Robert Sokolowski, *Introduction to Phenomenology* (Cambridge: Cambridge University Press, 2000), p. 168.

11 Ibid., p. 167.

12 Ibid., p. 176.

13 Hans-Georg Gadamer, *Heidegger's Ways* (Albany: State University of New York Press, 1996), p. 105.

14 Ibid., p. 107.

15 Sokolowski, *Introduction to Phenomenology*, p. 176.

Suggested reading

Paolo Berdini, *The Religious Art of Jacopo Bassano: Painting and Visual Exegesis* (Cambridge: Cambridge University Press, 1997).

Nicholas Davey, *Unquiet Understanding: Gadamer's Philosophical Hermeneutics* (Albany: State University of New York Press, 2006).

Ian Heywood and Barry Sandywell (eds) *Interpreting Visual Culture: Explorations in the Hermeneutics of the Visual* (London: Routledge, 1999).

Glossary

Abstract Expressionism
A form of art, dating from the USA in the 1940s, where abstract art is combined with Impressionism as an expression of the artist's feelings.

Altarpiece
A picture or carving depicting a religious subject and displayed above or behind the altar.

Apologia
A statement in defence of a particular belief; St Justin's *Apologia* was written to persuade the Roman emperor that it was wrong to persecute the Christian community.

Apse
A semi-circular section of the sanctuary, at the east end of a church beyond the altar.

Banderole
A small ornamental streamer or ribbon-like scroll bearing an inscription.

Boss
A keystone in the ceiling, holding the stone ribs in place but also having a decorative function.

Byzantine art
The art produced in the eastern Roman Empire from the fifth century until the fall of Constantinople (formerly Byzantium) in the mid fifteenth century.

Capital
The top of a column or pillar, often highly decorated.

Catacombs
Underground burial chambers, as used by the early Christians; they were usually in the form of passages with recesses for tombs.

Catechism
A summary of the teachings of the Christian Church.

Chancel
The eastern part of a church, where the clergy and choir sit.

Chantry
A chapel where the priests would chant Masses for the souls of the dead, particularly the benefactor who had funded the building of the chapel.

Christology
The study of Christ, particularly his nature as both God and man.

Counter-Reformation
The period of Catholic revival from the mid sixteenth to the mid seventeenth century which followed the Protestant Reformation.

Cubiculum (pl. *cubicula*)
A burial chamber within the catacombs.

Didache
A collection of very early writings (end of the first century CE) describing the traditions of various Christian communities.

Diptych
Two small works of art, joined together by a hinge so that they could be folded like a book; thus they could form a portable altarpiece.

Ecclesiology
The study of the Church as an institution.

Epigraphy
The study of inscriptions.

Epistemology
The philosophical theory of knowledge.

Eschatology
The study of the four 'last things': death, judgement, heaven and hell.

Exegesis
The explanation or expansion of a passage of Scripture.

Fathers
Influential early Christian writers and teachers, particularly in the first five centuries of the Church's history.

Fresco
A wall or ceiling painting, done while the plaster is still damp.

Hermeneutics
The study of the interpretation of religious texts, notably the Bible.

Iconography
The use of drawings to describe or illustrate a subject.

Impressionism
A style of painting that concentrates on the general impression produced; it developed chiefly in France in the late nineteenth and early twentieth centuries.

Lancet window
A tall narrow window with an arch at the top.

Loggia
An open-sided vaulted gallery.

Lunette
A half-moon-shaped space.

Mandorla
An almond shape formed by the intersection of two overlapping circles.

Nave
The main part of a church, where the congregation sits.

Orans
The praying figure.

Orthodox
The family of Christian churches, mostly in Eastern Europe, which separated from the Roman Catholic Church in the eleventh century.

Paleo-Christian
Relating to the time of the early Christians.

Pentateuch
The first five books of the Bible.

Pietas
A sense of duty or respect for an ancestor.

Post-Impressionism
A school of art developed in Europe during the late nineteenth and early twentieth centuries, developed from Impressionism but concentrating on the artist's reaction to a subject rather than the observer's view of it.

Pre-Raphaelite
In the style of a group of nineteenth-century British artists who aimed to return to a true representation of nature, as in art before the time of the Italian painter Raphael (1483–1520).

Renaissance
The revival of art and learning that began in Italy in the fourteenth century, continuing through the fifteenth and sixteenth centuries and spreading across Europe.

Reredos
An ornamental screen covering the wall at the back of an altar.

Sanctuary
The most sacred area of a church, where the altar is placed; usually at the east end of the building.

Sarcophagus
A stone container for a coffin or body.

Semiotics
The study of human communication, particularly words and the ideas they represent.

Septuagint
The ancient Greek translation of the Jewish Scriptures.

Sepulchre
A tomb.

Soteriology
The doctrine of salvation.

Spandrel
A wall space above and between arches.

Trecento art
Art produced in Italy during the fourteenth century.

Triptych
Three paintings hinged together, with the central painting flanked by two, less important side paintings; the standard form for altar paintings from the Middle Ages.

Vetus Latina
All those biblical texts translated into Latin that are not found in the Vulgate.

Vulgate
St Jerome's fifth-century translation of the Bible into Latin.

Index